The Way

of

Renewal

GS Misc 533

The Way

of

Renewal

A Report by the Board of Mission
of the General Synod
of the Church of England

CHURCH HOUSE
PUBLISHING

Church House Publishing,
Church House,
Great Smith Street,
London SW1P 3NZ

ISBN 0 7151 5542 3

Published 1998 for the Board of Mission of the General Synod of the Church of England by Church House Publishing

This report does not constitute an authoritative statement of the Church of England but is published solely as an aid to study by the Board of Mission of the General Synod.

Acknowledgements

Page 5: Extract from T.S. Eliot, 'The Hollow Men', in *Collected Poems 1909-1962* is reproduced by permission of Faber and Faber Ltd.

Page 41: Extract from 'We shall go out with hope of resurrection' by June Boyce-Tillman is copyright © Stainer & Bell and Women in Theology from *Reflecting Praise*.

Pages 7, 9, 36 Extracts from the Revised English Bible are copyright © Oxford University Press and Cambridge University Press 1989.

Page 37: Extract from The Book of Common Prayer, the rights in which are vested in the Crown, are reproduced by permission of the Crown's Patentee, Cambridge University Press.

Page 70: John L. Bell and Graham Maule, 'A touching place' is copyright © 1989 the Wild Goose Resource Group (The Iona Community, 840 Govan Road, Glasgow G51 3UV, Scotland).

Cover designed by Image-On Artworks
Printed by The Cromwell Press Ltd., Trowbridge, Wiltshire

Contents

Foreword

Rt Revd Nigel McCulloch, Bishop of Wakefield

The word 'renewal' has been increasingly prominent in church circles recently. Indeed, the Board of Mission, when it established the Mission, Evangelism and Renewal in England (MERE) Committee, was so concerned to see renewal on the agenda of the Church at this time that it deliberately included the word in its title – so that it could be seen to be a close and natural companion of evangelism. It has been the experience of many churches that evangelism is often carried out most effectively when a church is experiencing renewal. In the first meetings of MERE, we discovered that an exciting range of renewal was being experienced right across the Church. Michael Mitton, during his eight years as Director of Anglican Renewal Ministries, has been closely involved with charismatic renewal in the Church of England. We have much to thank God for in this injection of spiritual life during recent years. However, as Michael Mitton points out in his Introduction, that has been only one expression of a much wider renewal going on across the Church.

This report attempts to demonstrate both the breadth and depth of that renewal. In a report of this size it is not possible to touch on more than a few stories. There are, of course, many other expressions of renewal which are not included here. But the stories recounted in these pages make one vital point clear – this remarkable spiritual renewal is something which those inside and outside the Church need to recognize and understand.

Renewal has little to do with churchmanship or traditions. Nor is it confined to particular ages or social groupings. It is greater than that. We are daring to believe that a sovereign work of God is going on at this time – and that it is quickening the spiritual heart of our Church. The gloom-mongers who revel in reports of church decline need to read these stories.

This report has been written not only to convey the good news of renewal, but also to provide doorways for those seeking a deeper experience of God in their lives. Our sincere hope is that what is recounted here will inspire many to put themselves in the path of renewal. Ours is a church which certainly has its wounds. It is also a church which, under God, undoubtedly knows a renewing work of the Holy Spirit; and because of that, it can look forward with confidence to its ministry and mission, in the name of Christ, during the next millennium.

Introduction

Michael Mitton

During the last quarter of the twentieth century the Church of England has witnessed a spiritual renewal as dynamic and powerful as any it has known previously. It has also been a renewal unlike any it has known. In the history of this Church, there have been some outstanding renewals. But despite their many positive aspects, these renewals usually served to reinforce a polarity of churchmanship within the Church. In fact, such renewals often began as reactions to a particular expression of life in the Church, and were in effect protest movements. When the high tide of the new spiritual life subsided, therefore, the renewal could all too easily harden into forms, dogmas and rituals espoused by a particular grouping within the Church. This is where the current waves of renewal are different.

In 1996 I attended the first meeting of MERE – Mission, Evangelism and Renewal in England – a Board of Mission committee whose role is clearly identified in its name. At this meeting, I asked the question, 'What do we mean by "renewal"?' The fruit of my question was that I was asked to produce a preliminary paper on the charismatic renewal. As Director of Anglican Renewal Ministries, a national organization set up to encourage charismatic renewal in the Church of England, I was well placed to make some kind of assessment of this renewal. I offered this paper to the next meeting, and the ensuing discussion was fascinating; the document precipitated a discussion which showed very clearly that there were many renewals going on in the Church at this time. The word 'renewal' has often been used as a shorthand word for charismatic renewal, which can unfortunately infer that this is the only renewal, or that it is the most significant renewal. What is certainly true is that it is a very prominent and vigorous renewal which has had an enormous impact on the life of the Church. (The Board of Mission published a paper on a particular expression of charismatic renewal in 1996

1

entitled *The Toronto Experience.*) But the exciting thing we discovered in our discussions was the realization that in these days we are witnessing in our Church a very wonderful release of the Holy Spirit of God, whereby individuals and churches are encountering new life in many different areas of Christian life and witness.

This is where the late twentieth-century renewal is different from all the others. This is, if you like, a 'something for everyone' renewal. It is not a renewal to reinforce a churchmanship or a dogma (though fallen human beings may well want to use it that way). It is a collection of renewals affecting every area of church life and showing no particular preference as to personality or churchmanship. Very generally, we are witnessing a gracious moving of God in our midst, whereby cold nominalism is being replaced by personal love for God and, most significantly as we approach the end of this Decade of Evangelism, Christian people are finding new enthusiasm for sharing their faith.

In this book I have selected nine themes that became prominent in our discussions about renewal. As a committee we were very aware that there were others, but in the space of a small book we can only offer a limited number of themes. A larger book would have had scope to include, for example, the inspiring Cursillo movement. It could also have described the impact made by the Archbishop of Canterbury's teaching missions and other national and diocesan initiatives. In chapter 9 we would have been able to have included other examples of 'mission on reverse'. Our hope, however, is that the reader will be inspired to explore these and other areas of renewal. The purpose of the book is to offer a description of a variety of renewals, in the hope that individuals and churches will discover doorways into renewal and will be encouraged to come forward to share their experiences. Without renewal the Church cannot survive. Whilst the traditions and values of our Church are still treasured, there is nonetheless a deep yearning to experience faith as personal, immediate and dynamic. Increasingly, church members are displaying an unwillingness to have a faith simply for Sundays and private use; they want their Christianity to be vital and relevant for the whole of life. Hence the quest for renewal.

Renewal is something God gives, it is not something we manufacture. Our part is to become open, as we walk by faith. We journey on the road, thereby putting ourselves 'in the way of renewal'. This is how we got to the title of this book, *The Way of Renewal*. This is a journey of exploration and experience. We felt that the most helpful way of presenting this report was to collect stories, personal accounts of how people have discovered particular doorways which have led them into a renewal of faith. Each chapter therefore includes three such stories. Whilst we endeavoured to be as fair and balanced as possible, it is inevitable that some may feel that their particular preference has been ignored. Once again, limitations of space prevent us from being comprehensive. But we do want to assure the readers of this report that there is no intention to give preference to the churches, organizations and societies mentioned in this book. The resources listed at the end of each chapter are only some of the many resources around, but we hope that they will serve as starting points.

Some of our stories are by members of MERE, but many have been recruited from outside the committee; some are written by people prominent in their own field; others are unknown except in their own local church and community. Each, however, has an authentic story that is worth telling. We have a mixture of men and women, young and old, black and white, catholic and evangelical and shades in between. The variety of contributors is in itself a testimony to the diversity of this spiritual renewal that is taking place.

All who write the stories of this book have explored, taken a few risks and been open to adventure. Those who refuse to adventure will find it hard to discover renewal. In fact, to use the phrase in its opposite meaning, they will get in the way of renewal. They will be a blockage to renewal in their own lives, and quite possibly in the life of their church. But those who are willing to explore, willing to discover something new in their Christian lives, willing to allow the gentle but fiery Spirit of God to bring changes to their lives, they will be on the way of renewal.

This many-stranded renewal has the most wonderful potential in our postmodern age. There may be gloomy stories of declining congrega-

3

tions and financial problems. But read the stories in the following pages, and I think you will agree with me and my friends on the MERE Committee who have been so much part of the writing of this book: while God continues to bring such renewal to our Church, we have every reason to rejoice, not with blind arrogance, but with humble assurance, that the God of the impossible is at work in our midst. 'We are an Easter people, and Alleluia is our Song.'

How to use this book

Each chapter begins with a short introduction of the theme, followed by three stories of renewal. There are then a series of questions to help you reflect on the theme and apply it to your own life. These can be used on your own or with a small group. There is no particular order to the chapters. The idea is that you can choose whichever one interests you. There would be many advantages to meeting together with a small group from your church and exploring these renewals together. You could choose, say, half a dozen, and study one each week. As you do so, it is very likely that some of the stories will speak to your situation. Our sincere hope is that by reading these stories, and reflecting on them with the help of the questions provided, you will discover a doorway of renewal that will suit the spirituality and culture of you, your church and the community where you live and bear witness to the love of Christ.

Theological Perspective

Anne Richards

> This is the dead land
> This is cactus land
> Here the stone images
> Are raised, here they receive
> The supplication of a dead man's hand
> Under the twinkle of a fading star.

In his poem, 'The Hollow Men', T. S. Eliot describes a state of spiritual dryness. The aridity of the 'hollow men', the 'stuffed men', is a state of paralysis in which things happen automatically, stripped of meanings. Life moves on towards death and the effort of doing seems too much when the effort of being takes away all the available energy.

Although as Christians we may not like to think so, this state of spiritual dryness can be all too familiar. We may find ourselves too busy or exhausted to make the efforts required to pray or read the Bible regularly and we may find going to church a matter of a routine duty, to be slotted in and got over, so that we can attend to other, more pressing, matters. Even if our lives are not stressed and crowded, we may still enter a state of spiritual inertia, in which God seems far away and the effort of trying to seek out the power of the divine in our lives seems too much like a futile occupation or too much like hard work. If we realize this, we may torment ourselves with guilt and a feeling of having failed God, and so dig ourselves still deeper into a rut of empty church-going and sterile prayer. Eliot says, again:

> Between the idea
> And the reality
> Between the motion
> And the act
> Falls the Shadow

We know how we want to act for God, but inertia sets in before we can muster the effort. We let it ride, procrastinate. In prayer, we acknowledge God's own gifts to us for the establishment of the kingdom, but the power and the glory are beyond us. All that belongs to the saints, to the leaders of the Church, not to us.

It is important to realize that there is nothing unusual or unnatural about feeling like one of these hollow beings. Jesus himself spent time out in the desert wrestling with temptation to give up the service of God (Matthew 4.1-11). Tired and hungry, we see him facing the distractions and the easy ways out that we all often face in the course of being a Christian. Again, in Gethsemane, we see the exhausted disciples asleep and inactive as Jesus struggles to face his destiny: the 'spirit is willing but the flesh is weak'. We also see Jesus ultimately, in his time of abandonment, wrung out and dried out as he speaks from the cross the words 'I thirst' (John 19.28). We all thirst sometimes and sometimes we feel as if we have given the last drop.

This is why the concept of renewal is important in the lives of all Christians. The trouble is, many people associate the word 'renewal' with expressions of charismatic renewal and have images of people speaking or singing in tongues, being 'slain in the Spirit', or exhibiting phenomena with which they feel uncomfortable. Yet charismatic renewal is only one manifestation of renewal as an activity of God's Holy Spirit, for it is not circumscribed by any particular outward expression.

What then is renewal? Simply, it is an answer to the sense of aridity and spiritual dryness which Christian people can experience. It is brought about by the presence of the Holy Spirit in our lives. We understand it as renewal because of the difference it makes to our appreciation of God and of God's actions in and through Jesus, and as analogous to whatever we take in which gives us energy and vitality for all our physical activities.

How then can we experience the Holy Spirit in renewal? We know that God's Holy Spirit is an agent of the *creatorship* of the Triune God. We see the Spirit moving in the creation of the world, when 'a wind from God swept over the face of the waters' (Genesis 1.2). The Hebrew word *ruach* indicates the Spirit by means of an analogy to a rushing wind affecting nature, or to breath which signifies life, so 'the Lord God formed man from the dust of the ground, and breathed into his nostrils the breath of life; and the man became a living being' (Genesis 2.7). By imagining the life-creating power of the Breath of God we can say that the Holy Spirit is able not only to create the quality of life from what is dusty and 'dead', but can restore, reconcile, remake and re-energize whatever has fallen into paralysis or inertia or whatever seems to have gone dead and meaningless.

The Holy Spirit also represents the *power* of God's will in our lives, so that we can experience new energy, creativeness, confidence in the ability to act and the ability to make new. So many of us feel a fleeting hope at new beginnings: we make resolutions at the New Year, we feel inspired at births and weddings, or at the start of a new job. But then so often resolutions are broken, the newness and the inspiration wears off and there seems to be no way of sustaining the enthusiasm. In renewal, the Holy Spirit is able to infuse creative energy. We see this especially in the Pentecost experience (Acts 2):

> And suddenly from heaven there came a sound like the rush of a violent wind, and it filled the entire house where they were sitting. Divided tongues, as of fire, appeared among each of them, and a tongue rested on each of them. All of them were filled with the Holy Spirit and began to speak in other languages, as the Spirit gave them ability.

To the idea of wind or breath is added the idea of fire, bringing light, life and energy into people's lives and inspiring them with ability to witness to others in an immediate and special way. Peter then stands up and testifies to God's actions in Jesus Christ, telling his listeners that Jesus has risen from the dead and bringing many to ask for baptism. In this way, the enthusiasm, the power and the chance of a new start percolate into the world as missionary effects. This is also a feature of renewal in the Holy Spirit: the experience bears fruit for others. It is not a self-limited experience, benefiting the individual alone.

The Holy Spirit also reminds us of the *glory and majesty* of God and all that God intends for us and for his world, and so gives us a new *vision* and a new *hope*. We often forget about the dazzling beauty of God's presence and forget that we may have access to moments of awe and wonder when some aspect of the transcendental is suddenly made known to us. For some of us this may be mediated by art, literature or music, or by something seen or heard in the natural world. For others it will come through prayer or meditation, an experience of healing or on a pilgrimage. In this way, however, the ordinariness with which we habitually endow the world we see can be swept aside into something visionary which sustains our hope and trust in the Lord.

People describe the experience of renewal in all kinds of different ways. T. S. Eliot talks about the flash of lightning, the rain coming after long drought and a midwinter outpouring of the Holy Spirit. Sometimes people talk of drinking-in the Spirit. Others experience it as an upwelling of deep emotion, like falling in love, although they mostly mean that these intense feelings operate at a deep spiritual level. There may be an experience of being filled, which is sometimes called consciousness of the indwelling of the Holy Spirit. For others, renewal is marked by a change to a more positive outlook, and the renewal of hope. The world may suddenly seem to be filled with possibilities. Others too, experience a forgotten sense of value, meaning and purpose which gives sense to their lives and helps them to want to know God in a deeper way. Renewal then marks an opportunity for the midwinter spring – a spiritual growth.

Renewal can be experienced through many different agencies. This book sets out to illustrate just some of them. Because all people are different, not all will lead to experiences of renewal. Part of a person's faith journey involves discovering which ways open them up to the outworking of the Holy Spirit and how to use these ways to open themselves up to God's will and intention for their lives.

Perhaps more than anything else, the experience of renewal puts us in touch with the overwhelming nature of God's presence among us and the superabundance of God's love. God's giving knows no bounds, is not rationed or meted out in little packages. Rather, it is through renewal that we can begin to appreciate the extent of God's love and mercy, which is so difficult to grasp when we are dry and sterile in our own lives and relationships.

As David Ford has reminded us (in the Bible Society's *Transmission*, Autumn 1997, and in his recent book *The Shape of Living*), the prophet Ezekiel was overwhelmed by a powerful vision and experience of God which revealed to him a power, a glory and a message which so filled him with its force that he sat amazed for seven days. Then he used his life as a witness to the message. The experience gave him purpose and directed him how to act. But it is also in Ezekiel that we hear the story of the dry bones (Ezekiel 37). In the valley of dry bones, Ezekiel is asked whether the bones can live. Then, as Ezekiel prophesies to the bones at God's command, the bones come together and rise up, and new life is breathed into them. It is a powerful resurrection image of restoration through the power of the Lord:

> And you shall know that I am the Lord when I open
> your graves, and bring you up from your graves, O
> my people. I will put my spirit within you and you
> shall live, and I will place you on your own soil; then
> you shall know that I, the Lord, have spoken and will
> act', says the Lord.

This shows us that renewal can be experienced individually, but also corporately. Whole communities can be turned around to find a new sense of mission and purpose for their worshipping lives and action within the local community. Just as the Lord can restore the chosen people of Israel, so the Christian witness of the Body of Christ can be given new energy and new hope through the creative power of the Holy Spirit.

Renewal, then, can be seen as an important factor in spiritual growth and in the corporate journey in the lives of churches and Christian groups. The dynamism of the Holy Spirit is given to us as gift, and we have only to open whichever door is appropriate for us and God *will* come in.

1

Renewal through spirituality

Introduction

One of the features of the cultural transition taking place in the West is a marked quest for spiritual depth. This is evident not only in the Church, but in the lives of the many outside the doors of the Church who are searching for meaning in life. Despite the collapse of what we knew as Christendom, there is still within the psyche of most British people a Christian memory which, albeit vague and confused, is nonetheless real. The tragic and untimely death of the Princess of Wales in 1997 caused millions to dip into whatever religious consciousness they could find, pouring into our cathedrals and churches, using language of 'pilgrimage' and 'shrine' and religious symbolism such as candles to express their grief. The growing fascination with the so-called 'New Age' movement is another indicator of the quest for spiritual depth. The millennium is being perceived as a truly extraordinary moment in history. Only a few have lived through a change of millennium, and those who journey through this historic moment will have an uprecedented sense of sharing in a world-wide moment of destiny.

The dominance of the modernism of the 1960s and 1970s prevented secular and Christian alike from delving into the past for resources for the present. However, the transition into postmodernism is far more favourable to the past, especially the long-distance past. It is the saints of old who are seen to hold deposits of wisdom to help us face the pressures of the present and calm our anxieties about the future. It is in this context of cultural shift that we see a fast-growing interest in spirituality. Regardless of denomination or churchmanship, Christian people are searching into many different expressions of Christian spirituality as a resource for personal renewal. In this chapter we shall look at three particular expressions which are proving very popular in the Church today.

Dr Elizabeth Culling introduces us to *Celtic spirituality*, the oldest of the spiritualities we explore in this chapter. Elizabeth was on the staff of St John's College, Durham, before becoming rector of a group of rural parishes near Beverley, North Yorkshire. She shares with us her own journey of discovery of the spirituality that was rooted in the Christian mission of the Celtic peoples of the fifth century AD onwards. This spirituality is beautifully down to earth, and has so much to say about ministry, mission and prayer in our current culture. *Revd Richard Davies*, Vicar of Eastleigh in Hampshire, introduces us to *Ignatian spirituality*. This spirituality, with is origins in the life and teachings of Ignatius of Loyola in the sixteenth century, provides spiritual disciplines, including directed retreats, which have been the means of spiritual renewal for thousands of Christians. *Laura Wass* is one of the younger contributors to this book and writes about her encounters with the *Taizé community*. Compared to Celtic and Ignatian spirituality, this is a much more modern expression which has emerged during this century. Nevertheless, it draws from ancient traditions and often adapts them to the modern context. As Laura testifies, this spirituality is immensely attractive to young people.

All three writers discovered a new way of loving and serving God through their encounters with these spiritualities. All they needed was a willingness to explore beyond their spiritual norm. Their stories are a testimony to the value of such exploration.

1. Celtic spirituality   *Elizabeth Culling*

All spirituality is based on the experience of God which arises from particular beliefs about what he is like interacting with a certain way of life. The early Celtic people who migrated to the British Isles were among the first to hear the gospel and become Christians. Their experience of God was thus closely connected with their lifestyle. Although we cannot speak of a pan-Celtic consciousness, we can discern common themes in the faith of those who lived in the Celtic regions of these islands. The Celts were a rural tribal people and their pattern of life was translated into the Church.

The basis of the Celtic Church was monasticism. The monastery was at the heart of the community and very often the converted head of the tribe became the abbot. From the monasteries, which were resources for the Church, the monks went to preach the gospel. They travelled great distances, establishing monastic communities wherever they went. Orthodox in doctrine, the Celts thus organized themselves differently from the Roman model of Christianity and this was the basis for conflict between them. They loved the Bible, copying it in beautiful manuscripts and learning it by heart. They were deeply trinitarian, a feature reflected in their prayers, which were often constructed on the basis of three. They met God in creation, though they were acutely aware that nature itself was often hostile and contrary. They took the supernatural seriously and expected God to act to put down evil and show his power to those who needed or doubted him. They were motivated to spread the gospel and sought to be completely open to going wherever the Holy Spirit chose to send them. Pilgrimage, an important motif in Celtic spirituality, was thus bound up with both the individual's search for God and the desire to share him with others. They recognized the need for redemption, and although their great high crosses spoke of Christ's victory, they remembered the cost and the hold which sin still maintained on human lives. So they developed an elaborate penitential system and could be extreme in their attempts to subdue the body through ascetic habits. God, to the Celtic Christian, was both immanent and transcendent. He was closer than the air we breathe, yet ruler of the wind and waves. Their prayers are perhaps the most attractive feature which draws people to them today. They spoke to God about everything and expected him to be interested in their concerns, whether rising in the morning and laying the fire, going on a hazardous journey, working through the day or resting by the hearth at night.

My encounter with Celtic Christian spirituality started some years ago. I was living away from the North-East for the first time in my life, training for the Anglican ministry. I had just completed a Ph.D. thesis on the English Reformation and although I retained my passion for church history and the conviction that it was vitally relevant for the Church today, I was not keen to open any books on the subject of the Reformation for a very long time!

Being at theological college is a strange experience at the best of times. People from all walks of life, with a wide age range, men and women, are thrown together and expected to be a loving, growing Christian community. What is more, most of us had left behind our familiar church fellowships and support mechanisms and launched out in faith and not a little apprehension. Looking back, that was a very 'Celtic' thing to do. The early Celtic Christians had a love of wandering. *Peregrinati* they were called – *wanderers*. They set out in their frail coracles, leaving all known securities and with no fixed destination in mind, to be blown by the wind of the Spirit to wherever God might lead them. They were open to God's Spirit and that presented a real challenge to me, for, like most people, my instinct when feeling insecure in a strange environment was to close up and cling on to old familiar ways.

Just before I left, a friend gave me David Adam's book, *The Edge of Glory*. I read it and loved it, not least because in the introduction the author described how the book began as a Lenten discussion group in a village on the North Yorkshire moors, and that was where all my childhood holidays had taken place. As I read about the early Celtic Christians I felt at home, as if I was reading about my own spirituality. This tied in with my sense of being away from my roots and also with a desire to understand better the Christian tradition in which I now lived and worshipped. I am in no way a Celt and no one in the twentieth century can claim to be an authentic Celt. One of the biggest challenges of any historical renewal movement within the Christian Church is to learn from it without descending into nostalgia or self-deception that we can create the conditions to make it happen again, 'just like then'. There are a number of significant similarities between our culture now and the culture in which Celtic Christianity thrived, but they are not the same and we must seek God's heart for today's world and its needs.

Celtic Christianity seems to accommodate the postmodern culture in which we operate today. This is both a strength and a weakness. Postmodernism gives us the opportunity to pick and choose what we like and discard the rest. It is very easy to recreate the Celts in our own image. Many Christians are suspicious of Celtic Christianity because it suggests New Age beliefs. Yet the clear orthodoxy of the early Celtic

Christians, and their love of the Scriptures, should make us wary of those who try to make the Celts into pantheists. I have found that talking about the Celts provides a bridge for people who are spiritually aware yet alienated from the Christian Church. Spirituality is almost fashionable and if it is important to start where people are, then church is not the place to start. Interest in roots, in the origins of culture and a vague desire to pray, however, may help people to be open to hearing the gospel and get started in the Christian life.

Comparison between the world of the first Christians in Britain and the situation of the Church today led to a renewal of my own understanding of mission and evangelism. The tireless zeal of someone like St Aidan was already familiar to me through the lives of other missionaries since the Reformation, but the attitude of the Celts towards the surrounding culture helped me to think more clearly about how we should approach the culture of the late twentieth century. The Celts embraced what was good while standing firmly against sin and evil. They have been criticized for accepting too much of the world, yet they were fiercely opposed to the practices of the druids; they healed sickness and warned those who rejected God of the consequences. Their all-encompassing approach to life, expressed so clearly in their prayers, is something which our own culture, with its deep splits and dualisms, needs to hear. Contemporary Christianity has often colluded in this splitting and needs to let go of the invidious divide between sacred and secular, matter and spirit. The Celts went to the people and lived among them. Aidan was noted for his gift of being able to speak to all whom he met. He was not limited by age or class and he demonstrated the love of Christ in practical ways as well as speaking about it. Here is a model of sharing the gospel which is vital for today, for people who are looking for integrity, community and something which works. In my role as a church leader I have discovered that I need models of mission which help our Church to think more clearly about her mission. Our setting is like so much of Western society: community is crumbling, people are individualistic in their way of life and increasingly distant from their Christian roots, yet wanting to belong. Celtic Christianity has helped me to take a fresh look at how we can best reflect the love of God together.

In our 'pick and mix' society even Christians have begun to select those aspects of Christianity which appeal and reject the difficult parts we do not wish to hear. Many facets of Celtic Christianity are relevant to our own situation. We hear a lot about Celtic affinity with the natural world and this clearly resonates with many people who are deeply concerned about the environment and our relationship with it. Here we have a way of counteracting the idea that Christianity is at best indifferent and at worst hostile to the natural world. Instead of overreacting and heading down the New Age road of worshipping the created world, the Celts show us a different way. We cannot pretend that the early Celts were 'green' Christians, but it may be a revelation to people with no Christian background that we can discover and worship the creator through creation.

The story of Celtic Christianity has come down to us through the long tradition of their poems and prayers, and through the lives of the Celtic saints. Both prayer and the example of other Christians were already part of my own evangelical tradition and the fresh input from these early saints expanded my understanding of how God dealt with his servants. The lives of Aidan, Cuthbert, Hilda and others are an inspiration for any age. These people trusted God and were faithful to him in a hostile world. They expected his Spirit to guide and direct them, and they knew a freedom which so many Christians have yet to discover. The prayers and poems, collected and reshaped, remind us that God is everywhere and may be encountered in all things. David Adam has provided anthologies of prayers which are rhythmic and memorable and which apply in a rich variety of ways. Using these prayers with small groups has been an enlightening experience. Many have rediscovered prayer through their simple everyday language and have been able to make it their own again. Celtic prayer is not a technique to be learned, as so many types of prayer purport to be. It is rather a way of bringing the whole of life into focus in the presence of God and living it there.

Many people expect to hear something very new and different when they listen to someone talking about Celtic Christianity. But for many, it simply affirms what they already know and experience. I once spoke to a group in Northumberland and invited questions and comments at the end. 'But isn't it just what we are doing anyway?' was the first puzzled response. Christians in the North-East of England are already familiar with much that is now termed 'Celtic'. Their churches are called St Hilda's or St Aidan's. They know the stories of the saints who brought the gospel to those regions, and they recognize the presence of Christ in their daily lives, whether working, travelling or at home performing ordinary tasks. We must keep on remembering that the Celtic Christians were orthodox believers, grounded in the Scriptures and expectant that God was with them and would work out his purpose for the whole of creation through their lives. Renewal through Celtic Christianity comes through grasping afresh the very old truths, and putting into practice some basic gospel principles. There are many people who have no idea what is meant by 'Celtic Christianity', but speak of meeting God at work, of God present and all-encompassing, God who is interested in the little details of life; and they will respond and relate to such a faith as something for them.

I have found it inspiring to return to the places associated with Celtic Christianity, particularly Holy Island off the Northumbrian coast, the base of Aidan and Cuthbert, and Iona, where the Iona community seeks to echo the radical Christianity of the early Celts in the modern world. Celtic Christianity is part of our Christian inheritance in the British Isles, and its echoes of an earlier way of being the Church challenge our own church life, calling us to be more authentically Christian, people of integrity, putting our faith into practice and demonstrating what it means to be community, the body of Christ.

2.   Ignatian spirituality *Richard Davies*

'I feel a need to come face to face with God; with nothing in between, nothing to get in the way!' That was the first concern I shared, some 11 years ago, with the person who had agreed to be my Spiritual Director. His response to my concern led me into a life-changing, heart-warming, exhilarating journey into God by way of Ignatian spirituality.

But it was not the first powerful experience of God in my life. After our wedding, my wife and I moved to the north of England to buy a house and set up home. We were welcomed into the local church by members of a prayer group who invited us to their meetings. For as long as I can remember I have attended church regularly; I joined the local church choir at the age of eight, and ever since my teens I have been interested in matters religious. But up to the time of joining this church and prayer group, religion had been something to read books about and debate, an interesting subject. But amongst this group of Christians in Yorkshire, for the first time in my life I had a personal encounter with God; an encounter that engaged other parts of my personality, my whole being and not just my mind; an encounter associated with very powerful feelings. And so my faith became personalized – a personal relationship with God had begun. This personal encounter with God has been a characteristic of all subsequent significant developments and growth points in my journey of faith and in particular my experience of Ignatian spirituality.

This experience in Yorkshire led me into an involvement with evangelical Christianity. This phase of the journey did not last long but I shall always be grateful for this personal encounter with God, a God who cares for me and is interested in the details of my everyday life. I am less grateful to the evangelical culture for the work ethic which, combined with some less helpful traits in my own personality, had the effect of making prayer hard work. In an attempt to become more faithful to the God I had newly encountered, to become a better disciple, I felt the urge to be 'busier' in my prayer. I filled up my 'quiet times' of prayer with more and more devotional activities: Bible reading with notes or commentary, saying the daily services of the Church, the prayerful reading of a daily newspaper, praying lists of intercessions, etc. I had so much to do that I found it hard to pack it all into the time I set aside each day for prayer. It was this that brought me to the concern that I shared with my Spiritual Director: all these prayerful activities, instead of bringing me closer to God, seemed to be getting in the way. I felt a need to come face to face with God – with nothing in the way.

One of the suggestions made by my Spiritual Director was that I might consider making an individually guided retreat in the Ignatian tradition instead of my customary preached retreat. An individually guided retreat usually lasts for eight days (a longer version lasts for thirty days) and the retreatant brings only a Bible, notebook and pencil. Each retreatant is assigned a guide for the retreat who is seen privately each day for up to an hour. The retreat is kept in silence apart from the conversation with the guide. Within each day the retreatant is invited to have several periods of prayer, each lasting about an hour. For each of these the guide suggests a prayer activity: a short passage of scripture, a poem, a picture for meditation, an imagination exercise, etc. The retreatant is invited to keep a simple record of what happens in the prayer period, particularly any moods or feelings encountered. These written reviews are shared each day in the session with the guide who, on the basis of what has come up, will suggest more prayer activities for the next day.

The suggestion seemed good to me, so I duly signed up for an eight-day individually guided retreat in London at the Royal Foundation of St Katharine's. I must say that I was mightily apprehensive. The thought of spending so much time on my own, and in silence, was daunting. I was nervous at the prospect of sharing my deepest thoughts with a stranger. I was frightened of loneliness and boredom. As I had expected, the first couple of days of the retreat were fairly painful! I set aside four periods of prayer each day with half an hour of review after each one. At first, the bible passages I was given seemed so short: after ten minutes I felt I had prayed out of them all I could! It was so hard to sit there for the full hour, but I persevered in the hope that soon something would begin to happen! In those first couple of days I impatiently watched the clock, waiting for mealtimes to come around. The highlight of those difficult days was the hour's walk I had scheduled into my timetable!

On the third day something did happen. Suddenly I seemed to settle. My mind, which had been so full of anxieties and the concerns of my life back at home, became much less distracted. I noticed that all the bible passages I had been given for my prayer times were about God's love. My guide had been encouraging me to listen carefully for God's word to me in these passages. During the first couple of days these passages had caused me to think – they had engaged my mind – but had left me largely unmoved. On the third day, however, when I was reflecting on

Isaiah 43.1-4, something different happened. In the passage God was addressing Jacob but my guide had encouraged me to substitute my own name for the name Jacob. So the passage ran:

> But now, Richard, this is the word of the Lord, the word of your Creator . . . Have no fear, for I have redeemed you; I call you by name; you are mine. When you pass through water I shall be with you; when you pass through rivers they will not over-whelm you; walk through fire, and you will not be scorched, through flames, and they will not burn you. I am the Lord your God . . . your deliverer . . . you are precious to me . . . you are honoured, and I love you.

Suddenly it seemed as if God was speaking directly to me. I wasn't just thinking about this passage, my whole being seemed suddenly to be engaged. A feeling of warmth, of peace, of security spread through my whole body. I felt loved by God and it was the most incredible feeling! Again, here was a personal encounter with God, an encounter which engaged my whole being. This was a turning point in the retreat. From then on I felt very much held in God's loving embrace while he showed me things about myself, about himself, and about my life in him. Now it seemed as if God himself was the retreat guide. I realized – and I have relearned this truth time and time again since then – that before any-thing can happen, before revelation can take place, before growth can happen, before learning can be received, there has to be a grounding in the love of God.

Henri Nouwen, a contemporary writer and teacher of the spiritual life, captures something of my experience in his book *In the House of the Lord.* He says this:

> [D]iscipline in the spiritual life means . . . a gradual process of coming home to where we belong and lis-tening there to the voice which desires our attention. It is the voice of the 'first love'. St. John writes: 'We

are to love . . . because God loved us first' (1 John 4:19). It is this first love which offers us the intimate place where we can dwell in safety. The first love says: 'You are loved long before other people can love you or you can love others. You are accepted long before you can accept others or receive their acceptance. You are safe long before you can offer or receive safety.' Home is the place where the first love dwells and speaks gently to us. It requires discipline to come home and listen, especially when our fears are so noisy that they keep driving us outside of ourselves.

In a nutshell, it is Ignatian spirituality which has enabled me to come home; to find that intimate place of love, of safety, of acceptance from which I can dare to face myself with all my anxieties, fears and illusions; and to face the ups and downs, joys and sorrows of daily living. As Henri Nouwen suggests, it is the staying in that place which is difficult. I struggle constantly with the demon voices of guilt and anxiety, the strident voices which drown out the 'still, small voice' of God; but Ignatian spirituality has shown me a way, a method, a *discipline* to help me to keep returning to that place.

For me the annual Ignatian retreat is now a deep, prolonged returning to that place, that home where I am secure in God's love. It is an experience I would find it hard to do without. But the retreat is only 8 days out of 365! During my normal daily living there are a number of other disciplines which help me to stay in that place. I try to have two periods of prayer each day. At the beginning of the day in my prayer I use whatever scriptural passages have been particularly helpful in bringing me back to my home in God's love. I simply rest in that place in preparation for what may lie ahead that day. At the end of the day my prayer involves reviewing the day: looking back over it, reliving it in my mind's eye, and trying to identify, by reflecting on moods and feelings, where God has touched me. In addition, I try to spend a full day each month in quiet with God at a local retreat centre where I pray, read, walk, relax in God's presence. All these ingredients form a kind of scaffolding for my life and help me to stay in touch with my 'home' in God's love, to recognize his concern for the everyday happenings of my life, and to discern where I fit into God's loving involvement with his world.

3.   Taizé spirituality   *Laura Wass*

Taizé is a community of brothers founded by Frère Roger during the war, originally to hide Jews. It has since developed as an international and ecumenical Christian community with a focus on reconciliation. Many young people travel from all over Europe and beyond to visit it during the summer. It is situated in Burgundy, about half way between Dijon and Lyon. The nearest town to Taizé is Cluny. In the summer there are regular week-long programmes of bible study, meditation, work, etc. There is a service three times in a day the Chapel of Reconciliation, before breakfast, lunch and after the evening meal. On each Friday there is a prayer around the cross and on the Saturday night there is a candlelit service. Approximately 6,000 people visit Taizé each week during the summer.

I first visited Taizé in 1993, when I was only twelve years old. My mother had heard about it through various sources, and we both thought it sounded interesting. At this time we knew virtually nothing about Taizé. We were not even sure exactly where it was, but we decided (quite spontaneously) to go. My father and younger sister decided not to come, but who could blame them? After all, we were taking a 'leap of faith' into the unknown!

The journey to Taizé took us about twenty hours, as we travelled across both England and France by public transport. At times we were not even sure how we were going to get there, but we made it, eventually. The whole thing felt like a real adventure to me; just my mum and me, with a backpack and a tent – who gets the chance to do that at twelve?

I had no idea what to expect of Taizé, but it exceeded even my wildest dreams! We arrived to find that approximately 6,000 young Christians were just arriving for a week, and about the same amount were leaving. Of those who were leaving, many were in floods of tears. I remember thinking, 'What is going on in this place?' It was amazing! What also shocked me was that the coaches which both brought people and took them away were from countries all over the world. There were people from Lithuania, Latvia, Russia, Poland, Scandinavia, all over Africa etc. Many places that I had not even heard of! I could not understand what had drawn people from across the globe to come to Taizé. I later found out from a Lithuanian lady, that it had cost her six months' wages to come, and that she and her family had at times lived off just coffee and bread, to save money for this trip.

I remember so clearly the first 'prayer' (service) I went to. There were about 6,000 people in the chapel. Everybody sat on the floor and the brothers knelt in an enclosed space down the middle. Around the edge of the permanent church were marquees, so that there was enough room to hold everybody. It is impossible to describe the atmosphere as you enter the church, but I can honestly say I have never felt closer to God than when I am in that church.

The prayer in itself I also find amazing. It is a completely unique style of worship. Firstly there are the chants. These are a sentence or two of scripture (in practically any language) which is set to music and then sung over and over. The words become a prayer – meaning you can meditate on a piece of scripture or just pray. The chants in themselves are also extremely beautiful pieces of choral music, with both instrumental and sung solos. A short piece from the Bible is also read out in many languages. After this follows a silence of about five to ten minutes. I find this brilliant for prayer, meditation, and also just listening to God. The first time I experienced the silence I found it both difficult (because I didn't know what I was supposed to do) and also uncomfortable, as church never had these silences. I was so used to the formality of services that when faced with free expression I was confused. I now find the free expression and time for my own thoughts uplifting. The silences in themselves brought renewal into my faith, because I was forced to try something new.

Another aspect of life at Taizé which I really enjoy is the discussion groups. When you go to Taizé, you can choose whether you want to spend your week (two sessions a day) in a working group (doing day-today jobs like cleaning toilets), in a choir group (learning more about the music) or in a bible study/discussion group. Through the discussion groups I have met people from all over the world and also gained a deeper understanding of the Bible. These groups allow an insight into other cultures and encourage a chance to hear different points of view. The 'usefulness' of these daily meetings depends entirely on your particular group. Some groups get on better than others! Also I have sometimes found the discussions a little challenging or difficult, but the majority of the time I have found them extremely interesting and beneficial. The groups also provide a platform off which brilliant friendships can be formed. I still keep in contact with many of the people I have met at Taizé over the years.

Friendships are also made through the social side of Taizé. The young people at Taizé cannot be accused of being boring! After the evening prayer, many people go to the Oyak, which is an open-air café. Behind it people play guitars, sing and generally have a good time. I really enjoy going to the Oyak – it gives the chance to relax and have fun, the chance just to socialize.

The aim of the brothers of Taizé is to provide an experience of a simple life which gives rise to meditation and reconciliation to God. The simplicity applies to the whole way of life during your stay. This includes camping (or barracks), simple food and cold showers! Some people find this way of living difficult and uncomfortable because they are used to today's luxuries. I find it refreshing!

I am now seventeen years old and have visited Taizé five times. It is difficult to put into words what draws me to this most spiritual place. The main reason is that I quite simply feel so close to God. Over the past I have been thinking about the direction of my life – both my studies and future career, but also the direction of my faith. In everyday life it is so easy to get caught up in work and other things that I have found myself drifting from God, not losing faith but not finding enough time just to be close to him.

At Taizé, with 'prayer' three times a day (which sounds a lot but the services are so different to the ones I have experienced before), it is so easy to be near God – both to talk to him, but also to listen. I have found this one of the most rewarding parts of going to Taizé. While I am at home it is so easy to feel isolated. Going to Taizé, with 6,000 other Christians, brings a renewal to my faith, as does the feeling of being so close to God.

For reflection

1. Which of the three spiritualities described above attracts you most?

2. What particular feature of that spirituality appeals to you?

3. Are there practical steps you can take to explore it further?

4. Reflect on Celtic Christian spirituality, perhaps going for a walk and becoming aware of God's creation. Turn your reflections into prayer and worship.

5. Reflect on Ignatian spirituality. Read Isaiah 43.1-4, and as Richard was encouraged to do, write your name in the place of Jacob's and use it to become open to God's love touching you.

6. Reflect on the spirituality of Taizé. Find a cross and a candle and spend some time in silence, meditating on the cross of Jesus and the theme of his bringing light into the world. You might like to buy a tape or CD of Taizé music and play this during your meditation.

Resources

Celtic spirituality

The books by David Adam are the best modern introduction to Celtic prayer and the Celtic vision of life.

Visits to places associated with the Celts are the best way to begin to understand who they were and how they lived. The address for the publications of the Iona community is: The Iona Community, Pearce

Institute, 840 Govan Road, Glasgow, G51 3UU (Tel: 0141 445461).

Anthony Duncan's *Elements of Celtic Christianity* (Element Books, 1992) is a simple but comprehensive introduction to the Celts.

Elizabeth Culling's own booklet, *What is Celtic Christianity?* (Grove Books, Spirituality Series No. 45) is a useful introduction.

Ignatian spirituality

More information about spiritual direction and retreats in the Ignatian tradition can be obtained from: The National Retreat Association, The Central Hall, 256 Bermondsey Street, London SE1 3UJ (Tel: 0171 357 7736; Fax: 0171 357 7724).

Taizé spirituality

Details of Taizé from: Taizé, 71250 Cluny, France (Tel: 0033 85 50 30 30; Fax: 0033 85 50 30 15).

2

Renewal through worship

Introduction

For many people, their doorway into renewal is an encounter with a new expression of worship. It is the Anglican Church which probably contains the widest range of styles of worship. Some express their worship of God through the solemn dignity of a cathedral evensong, while others prefer the relaxed informality of a modern charismatic service. Some will dance in the aisles, whereas others prefer to sit in contemplative silence. Some love the language of ancient liturgies and prayers, while others prefer spontaneity and extempore prayer. At best, this diversity brings great richness to our Church; at worst it gives rise to prejudice and suspicion. But as we prepare to enter the next century and another era of Christian witness, perhaps we can dare to believe that we are moving away from the old intolerances and polarizations, into a new period of respect and exploration.

Our three contributors to this chapter demonstrate such exploration. Each writes of a new discovery in worship. This discovery has not resulted in the abandonment of their 'old' way; rather, they have sought to integrate their discovery into their worship, and this has been for them a doorway of personal renewal. There are so many aspects to renewal and worship that it is frustrating to confine ourselves to just three stories. However, our three writers cover three areas of worship which are undoubtedly having a vitally renewing influence on our Church today: charismatic renewal, liturgical renewal and world worship.

Revd John Leach was the vicar of a thriving evangelical church in Coventry before becoming Director of Anglican Renewal Ministries in 1997. He comes originally from an evangelical experience of worship and describes in this article the changes that have taken place in his life as a result of his encounter with charismatic worship, not least a holistic integration of his emotions into his worship life.

The Revds Dhoe and Peter Craig-Wild are ordained Anglican priests currently working in the Diocese of Wakefield. Dhoe is Priest-in-charge of Bruntcliffe in South Leeds and Rural Dean of Birstall, and Peter is Vicar of Mirfield near Huddersfield. Much of the story relates to when they were working as curate and vicar respectively of Chapeltown in Sheffield. Dhoe also worked as assistant Diocesan Director of Ordinands and Peter as Rural Dean of Tankersley. Both of them have their roots in the liberal/catholic tradition of the Church, but in recent years they have been involved in charismatic renewal. In their story they explain how they have come to believe that the Church's liturgy provides the most effective framework for the Holy Spirit to bring renewal to the people of God. Both John and the Craig-Wilds share the conviction that it is quite possible to integrate the beauty and dignity of liturgy with the freedom and spontaneity of charismatic renewal.

Martin Conway is a lay member of the Church of England who has had a career with the world-wide ecumenical movement, often participating as a simultaneous interpreter at the World Council of Churches conferences. He was President of the Selly Oak Colleges, Birmingham, until his retirement in 1997. From his experience of worshipping in many different traditions and cultures, Martin sees a great potential for renewal in the growing awareness of the many expressions of worship around the world. He touches on the influences of such places as Taizé and Iona and appeals to us to learn from the 'indigenous cultures' of the churches in the South.

1.   Charismatic worship   *John Leach*

It isn't always love at first sight. In fact it can often be the case that what you later come to love passionately you begin by hating thoroughly. As a twenty-something Baptist attending my first charismatic service at St Paul's, Hainault, Essex, under the leadership of Trevor Dearing, I realized that I disliked charismatic worship and Anglicanism with almost equal vehemence. Now look at me! It wasn't that I was a traditionalist. Those interminable Baptist hymns bored me stupid, and as a member of After the Fire (a Christian rock band) I was well used to more contemporary musical expressions. The charismatic ditties of the early seventies seemed to me at the time musically banal. But that wasn't the real problem. It was the way people sang them. They put everything into it, minds, spirits, emotions and, more disturbingly, bodies. It was almost as if they were enjoying it! I had sung a lot of hymns and played a lot of music, but if this was really worship I had certainly never done it before, and I certainly never wanted to do it again.

But I found, paradoxically, that the more I was turned off emotionally, the more convinced I became intellectually. The church life I saw lived out before me at St Paul's, and later in other churches, seemed to me to be exactly what a New Testament church would have looked like. I watched myself in bemused wonder as I kept going week by week to services I knew I would hate. Like the theologian Rudolph Otto, I had discovered the *mysterium tremendum et fascinans*, the terrifying but fascinating mystery of God which scares you silly but keeps you coming back for more.

But it was in a very different setting that I think I became a charismatic convert. My home church had a faith-sharing visit from Barry Kissell and a team from St Andrew's, Chorleywood, and I can remember walking by accident into a room where the team was meeting before the start of the day's activities. They were singing a worship song, quietly, gently and reverently, but with such sincerity and beauty that I was moved to tears. At that moment I performed a mental flip which made charismatic renewal, and the charismatic worship which was a symptom of it, things to be sought after and desired rather than feared and avoided.

However, this didn't solve everything; in fact, it created more problems. Wanting to be a charismatic didn't of itself make me one, and my paranoid dread of people who put their arms in the air didn't vanish overnight. The next few years were passed in a rather schizophrenic manner as I pursued my love/hate relationship with renewal worship.

Embarrassed beyond measure when we sang anything remotely 'charismatic' in church, I would feel like a wistful spectator as I watched others doing properly what I secretly longed for but just couldn't bring myself to do. I can remember the first time I ever dared to lift my hands in worship: it was at my ACCM (now called ABM) selection conference at a convent in Woking. I had since become an Anglican (that's another story) and was testing out a call to ordained ministry. I was far away from home among people I would probably never see again, and the feeling which followed, of delicious naughtiness and incredible exhilaration, felt like a cross between learning to swim for the first time and smoking my first (and only) joint as a student. I don't understand why some people are so hung up about showing their worship physically, but I do know what it feels like, and the feeling of liberation which followed this simple physical act was life-changing. I think it had become an issue over which I had said to God, 'So far but no further', and as such it symbolized a much deeper malaise. I'm not convinced God is that bothered about where we put our hands (within reason, of course), but he is bothered about our hearts and wills. We seldom find peace and true freedom in God whilst we keep boundaries up.

I didn't become embarrassingly liberated after this, but I did gradually become free: free to express my worship physically or not as I felt appropriate. As I became more at ease with renewed worship I relaxed into charismatic spirituality too, and began to experience some of the gifts for which charismatics are (in)famous. My pilgrimage continued with three further breakthroughs in my experience of renewal worship. The first came, as did so many other breakthroughs, with the ministry of John Wimber, the Californian leader of the Vineyard Church. I did not (and still do not) much like Vineyard-style music, but I did learn that one object of worship is intimacy with God. Charismatic worship began to touch my heart and emotions in a way that the hymns of my childhood had seldom done, and through the singing of worship songs I began to learn to express a deep love for God and desire for more and deeper communion with him. I saw this too in the people among whom I ministered, and I rejoiced in the spiritual growth, particularly among those new to the faith, through the medium of the worship song culture.

The second breakthrough came in the area of liturgy. It was the liturgy of the Church of England, rather than its music, which first attracted me, but I began to find a deep spirituality through the combination of charismatic songs and Anglican set texts. I was privileged for a while to be on the staff of a church where there was a tremendous amount of creativity, and we worked hard at combining these two streams in some exciting ways. I also began to experience the power of worship that was so evidently infused by the Holy Spirit. John Wimber taught the Church to recognize the 'coming' of the Holy Spirit in times of ministry, but I realized that the Spirit was often manifestly present when an expectant congregation gave itself to worship. People would be spontaneously healed as we sang; God might speak prophetically, or deal with people in significant, though gentle and private, ways during worship. This sense of a life-changing encounter with God became addictive: it simply wasn't enough for me any more just to sing songs or hymns about God without actually meeting with him. I had to learn, of course, to give myself to worship even when I didn't particularly feel anything, simply because God is worthy of worship, and this offering of a sacrifice of praise remains important. But there were still many times when I was conscious of having met profoundly with God. As a worship leader I became aware of the need to facilitate this meeting for the people I was serving. This expectation of encounter was again in stark contrast to the hymn-singing of my youth, which seemed in retrospect to have been much more about informing the mind than meeting the living God in an experiential way.

The third breakthrough was in the area of emotion. I had long been one of those people who are deeply affected by music of all kinds: I could easily find myself moved to tears by just about anything from Bach to Clapton. But more and more I would experience (and see in others) the same emotional stirring through worship music. I had to understand what exactly was going on when I suddenly burst into tears, or experienced shivers down my spine. This led me to research the whole area of music and emotion, and I began to understand how and why music can affect people emotionally. But as I moved into the world of charismatic renewal, I began to find my emotions touched through the music in a way which seemed directed towards God. I would find that emotional release led inevitably to an outbreak of praise to God as well as to the particular musician or composer. The greatest trigger for emotional stimulation, I discovered, both from my own experience and from academic research, is creativity: music which is samey and predictable affects people much less than music which has some element of surprise or a new twist to the harmony or melody. I am currently learning, as a musician, to use this knowledge to facilitate worship which touches the emotions, although I am also aware of the dangers of unhelpful manipulation of worshippers.

Charismatic worship and music can still, at their worst, be nothing more than twee little ditties with theologically inept (if not downright heretical) words. But I have discovered that at best it can facilitate a real encounter with God, based on scriptural truth, mediated through the liturgy, and leading to profound praise and life-changing effects. I'm still growing and learning, but I thank God from my heart for the renewal which has come to me through the work of liturgists, poets and musicians who are not afraid to be truly, no-holds-barred, open to the creative power of the Holy Spirit of God.

2. Liturgical worship *Dhoe and Peter Craig-Wild*

It was our first Ash Wednesday in Chapeltown. We had always used the imposition of ashes, and this night was no different. One by one people came to the altar rail and knelt down. We made the sign of the cross in ash on their foreheads, prayed the appropriate words, and they returned to their seats. It was a meaningful but not startling ceremony. As one person came forward Peter felt a compulsion to pray with her in more than just the formal way that had marked the ministry to that point. However, he balked; he didn't follow the prompting, but realized that there could be far more to this ceremony than he had ever appreciated.

The following year was different. The congregation had been taught that the imposition of ashes was more than just a formal ritual; it was an engagement with God through the Holy Spirit. As people came forward each person received the laying-on of hands, the Holy Spirit was invited to come upon them and manifest himself in and through the prayer. The charismatic gift of prophecy was used and prophetic words were shared with them and, at the end, the sign of the cross was made on the forehead of each one. The effect was dramatic. Many people were deeply moved and the Holy Spirit made the love of God more real than some had believed possible. One woman, who had been involved in charismatic renewal for some time, said that it was one of the deepest experiences of God she had ever known. After that, Ash Wednesday became a high spot of the year in Chapeltown.

Both of us had come into an experience of charismatic renewal in 1985. Jesus became more real; we rejoiced in a new-found freedom in worship and confidence in ministry; and we found support and encouragement from others involved in the renewal movement in Leeds. We owe a great spiritual debt to many people. But somehow there was always a sense of being fish out of water in the predominantly evangelical culture of renewal. We were both from a moderate catholic background, and the suspicion of liturgy and theology which seemed to mark much of the practice, if not the teaching, at renewal meetings made us feel quite uncomfortable.

People spoke freely about the renewal of worship, by which they seemed to mean either the rejection of Anglican liturgy and sacraments in favour of the more hidden liturgical patterns of Pentecostalism, or the 'livening up' of sacramental worship by the addition of the 'worship' or 'ministry' time. Only a few people, and not including ourselves at that point, seemed to grasp that the very power of the Holy Spirit for which charismatics longed was actually there within the sacraments themselves. It was only after our experience of Ash Wednesday in Sheffield that we began to think that the renewal of Anglican worship was not primarily about creating a new (evangelical) culture of worship but about freeing the intrinsic power of the sacraments themselves.

Peter was always self-conscious about the Maundy Thursday Eucharist. Re-enacting the washing of the disciples' feet and stripping the church of all its ornamentation always seemed to fall short of the dramatic impact he thought it should have. But when these ceremonies are seen with new eyes – with the expectancy that the Spirit brings – they take on a more immediate significance. One year we had a number of people who had left the local house church and joined the Anglican Church. It was their first Maundy Thursday. Peter was particularly concerned that they would find the rituals of the Maundy Thursday Eucharist esoteric to say the least. Instead, at the end of the service they were moved to tears by what they had seen and experienced. The ritual of the service had made real to them, in a way never previously experienced, the devastation which Jesus must have felt on the day before he was crucified. This convinced us that the liturgy and ritual of our Church have an intrinsic power which is limited only by our familiarity and lack of expectancy.

Many Anglicans seem to experience little depth, meaning and power in the sacramental worship of the Church. Consequently, when their faith is renewed, they want either to jettison liturgy altogether or find ways of 'livening it up'. It was slowly becoming clear to us that the real way to renew the liturgy of the Church was to discover the power *within*, rather than seeking ways of adding power from *without*.

For many charismatic Anglicans there is the assumption (and, it must be said, the experience) that the Eucharist is the least helpful form of Sunday worship for a church that wants to grow. The theory is that the Eucharist is exclusive and therefore alienating, wordy and therefore boring, sacramental and therefore beyond the understanding of most people. The question must be asked: does the fault lie with the Eucharist, or with the way we understand, explain and celebrate it? What has happened to Wesley's insight that the Eucharist is a 'converting ordinance'? His experience among the hard-bitten working classes of his day was that the Eucharist was *the* act of worship that led people to the point of conversion.

Wesley's experience was echoed to some extent in Chapeltown. The Parish Communion was *the* growing service. It increased in size from about 70 people to 150. Eventually we had to create an extra service. It was not 'livened up' nor did we add extra 'worship' or 'ministry' bits to it, but we tried to enter more fully into its inner dynamic. For example, the Gloria is simply formalized praise; so it was liberated and extended, to allow the natural exuberance of that part of the service to flow. The Confession was at times opened out so that it became an opportunity for people openly to declare the sins of our Church, world, and community. These declarations occasionally acted as charismatic 'words of knowledge', when a sense of conviction would result from a word spoken by someone else. At the Proper Preface in the ASB Eucharistic Prayer (beginning 'and now we give you thanks . . .') the congregation could offer their own words of thanksgiving and praise. We quickly came to the conclusion that the Eucharist does not need any additions to enliven it – rather we need to rediscover the power that is there by the grace and ordering of God.

We discovered that the same is true of all the traditional liturgies of the Church: all the elements are there for us to enter more deeply into a renewing experience of God through the Holy Spirit, if we would only believe in what we are doing. Our first real involvement in the so-called 'Toronto Blessing' came through a highly liturgical act of worship. We were leading a weekend for a charismatic evangelical church in Sheffield. The subject was 'Praying with Symbols and Liturgy', and we had planned a special service for the Saturday evening. It was largely wordless and used icons, incense, movement, Scripture, candles, silence, quiet music and anointing with oil. All went well in terms of introducing a group of about 40 people to a completely new style of worship – that is, until we came to the time set aside for personal ministry. The intention was for people to come forward, receive anointing with prayer, and then return to their places. What happened was quite different. The very first person came forward, was anointed and then fell to the ground; then the second; then the third, until the floor was littered with people resting in the Holy Spirit. Some were simply lying quietly; others were weeping; still others were writhing as if in pain. There were a few who remained upright, but even they seemed to be experiencing something of the power of the Spirit upon them. And all this in what was supposed to be an introduction to contemplative prayer and worship! These services became a standard part of our renewal tool-bag.

The culture of renewal often implied that the Spirit would only 'come' when called down in a 'ministry time'. Our experience was that God comes by his Spirit upon individuals and the gathered community just as powerfully in a liturgical setting. Two stories from the Old Testament illustrate this. The first is the service at the centre of the dedication of Solomon's temple in 2 Chronicles 5.11-14.

> When the priests came out of the Holy Place (for all the priests who were present had hallowed themselves without keeping to their divisions), all the levitical singers, Asaph, Heman, and Jeduthun, their sons, and their kinsmen, attired in fine linen, stood with cymbals, lutes, and lyres to the east of the altar, together with a hundred and twenty priests who blew trumpets. Now the trumpeters and the singers joined in unison to sound forth praise and thanksgiving to the Lord, and the song was raised with trumpets, cymbals, and musical instruments, in praise of the Lord, because 'it is good, for his love endures for ever'; and the house was filled with the cloud of the glory of the Lord. The priests could not continue to minister because of the cloud, for the glory of the Lord filled the house of God.

This was some service, a great national event, the equivalent of a royal wedding; and the Holy Spirit entered in and affected the whole gathered assembly to the point where the priests could not continue.

The second story comes from the life of the prophet Isaiah; it is the prophet's call recorded in chapter 6 of his book: 'In the year that King Uzziah died I saw the Lord seated on a throne, high and exalted, and the skirt of his robe filled the temple.'

In this well-known story Isaiah was worshipping in the temple, almost certainly in a very ordered liturgical service, and through it he was transported to heaven. Both these stories tell us that the liturgies of the Church can affect both individuals and communities if only we would raise our expectations and deepen our awareness of what God wants to do and can do through them.

The womb of the Church's liturgy was the synagogue, but its nursery was the post-Pentecost Church. The historic liturgies of the Church were born out of the first Christians' struggle to come to terms with and deepen their experience of the Holy Spirit. Isn't it logical to assume that those liturgies developed and became central to the life of the Church because they succeeded in their task?

Over the past few decades the renewal of the liturgy has been a major item on the Church's agenda and has led to the production of many new rites. These have focused mainly on language and structure, and while the importance of this task is not to be underestimated, perhaps the real task is to discover the dynamic of the Eucharist and other rites, and learn how to enter more fully into them.

3.   Worship in and for the world   *Martin Conway*

This story, which I would like to subtitle, 'A Quantum Leap in Truth and Joy', has two origins: one distant in my student days 40 years ago; the other much more recent and still very much under way. As a young and rather earnest student, I recall becoming increasingly bothered by the repetition, over and over again at successive communion services, of Cranmer's words in his prayer of confession:

> We acknowledge and bewail our manifold sins and wickedness, Which we . . . most grievously have committed . . . We do earnestly repent, And are heartily sorry for these our misdoings; The remembrance of them is grievous unto us; The burden of them is intolerable.

Was this really something I could honestly say?

I rejoiced to hear Mervyn Stockwood once cry out to an undergraduate audience, when a question was raised about the seriousness of someone's sin: 'Oh, for goodness' sake, don't harp on your sins; they're mostly far too petty for God to be bothered about.' But a deeper understanding dawned when I heard someone say – I forget who, but it may well have been Hugh Montefiore:

> The whole point of corporate worship is that Christians are representing before God not just themselves but the wider world of which we are a part. Pray that prayer about children dying of hunger in Ethiopia, or about the number of fatal car accidents on the roads.

That grew into the realization that there is a vital symmetry between mission and worship as the always dual obedience of those who are called into Christ's body, his Church. Just as it is the proper, indeed unique, task of Christians to represent the good news of God to their neighbours in mission, so it is our equally proper, indeed unique, task and duty to bring the joys and pains and sorrows of the wider world to God on behalf of our neighbours in worship. Ever since, this reference to the wider, worldly, secular community has been for me a litmus test of the truth and reality of worship.

Much more recent, and still far too little known, let alone followed, is the astonishing renewal of worship that has been taking place at the conferences of the World Council of Churches, starting from its Sixth Assembly in Vancouver in 1983. I know of nothing so vivid in its realism and piercing in its joy as this tradition at its best. There is not the space here to tell the story at length, from its origins in Vancouver to the striking series of morning services at the World Mission Conference of 1989 in San Antonio, Texas, and the Seventh Assembly at Canberra in 1991. The story has continued in the rather less successful experience of the World Conference on Faith and Order at Santiago de Compostela in 1993; and most recently in several unforgettable acts of worship at the 1996 World Mission Conference at Salvador de Bahia, Brazil. I shall use this last to convey something of the excitement and inspiration of this tradition, which is evidently still developing.

The first, startling and vital 'balance' in this tradition, secured by the many different people who shared in creating it, is that worship offered and patterned for the sake of the whole world can also be entirely specific to one particular group of people gathered at one particular time and place. At the Salvador conference the most important, true and moving occasion, mentioned in all the reports that I have seen, was the Saturday morning when we were all taken by bus to what I had earlier, on a walk through the city, taken to be some sort of aristocratic farmhouse by the sea's edge, now turned into a museum of modern art. That observation was true, but the deeper truth of that house and group of buildings is that its dock was where the first shipload of slaves from Africa was unloaded in 1550, and continued to be for over 300 years.

As we left the bus, we were given a service sheet which began with a guided meditation to be done in silence. This took me and the 500 others to the various parts of the complex, and so into a distant experience of what it means to be disembarked (an average of 40 per cent of the Africans would have died in the ships' holds, and at the time of disembarking, some tried to run away, others chose to throw themselves into the water), classified into humiliating categories (of which the 'objects' would have hardly understood a word), sprinkled with water in front of a building set apart (in fact, a sacramental baptism to increase the value of the 'cargo'), and then auctioned individually, with children separated from their mothers, for labour in the sugar cane plantations or wherever their 'masters' took them. We were invited, as a tiny sign of solidarity, however distant, to dip our hands in the sea, taste the salt water, touch our faces with it and feel the salt dry.

The ensuing act of worship proved exactly right for this quite specific occasion, when Christians from all over the world gathered at the dock of such cruelty and shame. The leadership was largely entrusted to the Afro-Brazilians (not least the magnificent drum band formed by forty or fifty of the abandoned street children) and the Africans from among whom the six million or more slaves had come. The President of the African Conference of Churches, Aaron Tolen from Cameroun, led us all in confession. A woman from Ghana brought a 'stone of tears' rescued by a local farmer when the old Portuguese fort on the erstwhile 'gold coast' was being restored. 'It represents 358 years of degradation,' she said; 'let it be a reminder that we will never do this to ourselves again.'

We were each invited, as part of the prayer, to follow a Salvadorian custom and receive from a neighbour a coloured ribbon round our wrist, and tie one round theirs, as a sign of enduring friendship and what the Spirit had conveyed to us that day. I was profoundly moved to find myself beside a delegate from the Church of Jesus Christ on Earth by the Prophet Simon Kimbangu (usually known, misleadingly, as 'the Kimbanguist Church'), which had so wonderfully received my eldest daughter on her gap year, and whose history is perhaps the outstanding example in this century of 'independent' African Christian initiative and missionary obedience.

The music of the service included three Afro-American spirituals ('Deep river', 'O healing river', and 'Oh, freedom'), a South African chant promising healing in the blood of the Lamb (sung in Xhosa) and, at the end, an Afro-Brazilian marching song, 'God calls the people now to a new life', whose rhythm and verve swept us all up into joyful commitment – and became the signature tune for the conference as a whole.

To put it in general categories, this was a magnificently imagined and composed act by the world-wide Church (in its representatives). It succeeded in bringing to God the awful heritage and experience of slavery endured by so many Africans and involving so many Europeans and others who had profited from it. We brought it to God precisely in order that God could in some mysterious way heal the sheer hurt and waste of slavery and its aftermaths, while also nerving the Church now to go out and turn those aftermaths into more humane and hope-filled possibilities for the descendants of the slaves and others whose fate today might prove comparably degrading – which was, of course, precisely what a World Mission Conference is all about. It was rightly an act of the universal Church. At the same time it was worship that could probably only have been properly expressed in the last fifty years by the group gathered for that particular conference that week. It integrated so much that was being felt and known and said in the rest of the conference.

A second characteristic of many of these renewed acts of worship has been the centrality of a content which cannot be exactly known in advance, because it is left to be created at the time by the participants. Sometimes this has been quite familiar: an invitation to all participants to think of someone who needs prayer, and then pray for her or him in a moment's silence. More often it has involved something rather more. In the Aids service, for instance, after a most effective mime/reading about the woman with an issue of blood, we were all invited to go forward to receive a red Aids ribbon from a basket in the aisles. The ribbon was tied around our wrist by the person in front of us. We then said to that person the name(s) of those we were praying for, and knelt and prayed by a long red cloth hanging from the arm of the great cross that had served all week as the centrepiece of worship. We sang June Boyce-Tillman's 1993 hymn 'We shall go out with hope of resurrection', to the 'Londonderry Air', which includes the words:

> We'll give a voice to those who have not spoken,
> we'll find the words for those whose lips are sealed; . . .
> We'll sing our songs of wrongs that can be righted,
> we'll dream our dreams of hurts that can be healed.
> We'll weave a cloth of all the world united
> within the vision of a Christ who sets us free.

Such words rang out in a way I could not have anticipated, true, costly and yet overwhelmingly joyful – not because of us but because of God's act in Christ. In our normal weekly acts of worship I have come to crave this possibility of leaders and arrangers deliberately providing space and setting for all those present there and then to think, share and indeed do something that we might well never have done without this specific expectation. This can vividly express the missionary obedience (i.e. related to the secular world out there) out of and into which the worship grows.

A third dimension of this renewal has been the way in which acts of worship can be actively planned and prepared so that they involve a much wider spread of the elements of our humanity. This includes the range of music used; I have found myself quite naturally and gladly singing liturgical responses in several languages and in the rhythms of other cultures than mine. I shall not quickly forget the tall Serbian – American priest with the darkest treacle voice I have ever heard, leading us into – and making altogether thrilling – a series of Byzantine responses to confession of sin and intercession.

Still more, the shape and style of the 'envelope' for worship has proved significant. We enjoyed that huge tent at the Vancouver Assembly with the back wall always open on to the world, and at Salvador the worship area was arranged diagonally into a high corner overlooking the wide, wide sea. At Vancouver the walls of the tent, provided with a bar at hand-height round all three sides, had been filled at the opening service by flags brought by all the delegates. For the closing service, these had been replaced by a myriad of children's drawings, each showing a child with its hands held out to the sides, so that they formed a circle of children holding hands around us. At the end of the service, as part of the sending out, we were each invited to take home one of these pictures and write to the child or class who had drawn it with an account of the Assembly.

Much care has also been taken with the look of these services, not least because they have so often been filmed for TV or video. This visual aspect has ranged from the striking reredos in the art of the local native North-West Canadians at Vancouver to the varied use made each morning at Salvador of the high, gaunt cross formed on a palm tree standing in the corner of that vast 'arena' on the cliff top.

Yet it is not so much the outer designing as the inner imagination and precision that has captivated my will and heart. The morning services at the San Antonio conference were each centred on the growth of a tree: starting with tiny, dry seeds, and moving through the experience of water in a dry land, the pruning of the tree, waiting for growth to happen, giving thanks for the joy of the fruit, and taking new seeds home with us to plant further fruit-bearing trees in our own places. At Salvador there was not this sense of a single story growing into its fullness day by day, but a similar truth and intensity in the biblical stories brought into prayer and action, into praise and thanksgiving for today and tomorrow.

You cannot talk about the realities of prayer and worship at a distance and in general terms; they are for experiencing and then living out. So a brief article like this is bound to be wretchedly inadequate, both in conveying the thrill of this still-developing tradition and for making it real in other settings. By definition, it cannot be a case of delegates to these conferences persuading their home churches to use these services. Their nature, thank God, has been such that they cannot simply be taken over. But what they can achieve is to inspire many different groups and churches to be as imaginative, as creative, as missionary in devising acts of worship that are specific to a specific time and place, yet no less universal in truth and intent.

One can really only say 'Go and do likewise' – as someone else used to . . .

For reflection

1.   Which of the three stories of worship described above attracts you most?

2.   What particular feature of that story appeals to you?

3.   Are there practical steps you can take to explore it further?

4.   Can you think of ways in which you and your church can experience the kind of holistic worship that John describes, involving not only the mind, but also the body and emotions?

5.   Are there ways in which you can encourage a more imaginative use of liturgy in your church, so that it becomes a renewing experience?

6.   What can you learn from Martin's story of learning from other cultures and nationalities? How could you encourage a greater cultural diversity in your church?

Resources

Charismatic worship

Write to: The Director, Anglican Renewal Ministries, 42 Friar Gate, Derby DE22 1DA (Tel: 01332 200175; Fax: 01332 200185; e-mail: armderby@aol.com).

Liturgical worship

The new liturgies to replace the ASB are to be called *Common Worship*: for further information contact Church House Publishing, Church House, Great Smith Street, London SW1P 3NZ (Tel: 0171 340 0274; Fax: 0171 340 0281; E-mail: info@chp.u-net.com). New lectionary provision and services of baptism and confirmation have already been published and the remaining new services will become available over the next few years following authorization by General Synod.

The following are compilations of material which have already been published with the new liturgies in mind:

Patterns For Worship, Church House Publishing, 1995.

Lent, Holy Week and Easter, Church House Publishing/Cambridge University Press/SPCK, 1984.

Promise of His Glory, Church House Publishing/Mowbray, 1991.

Enriching the Christian Year, Mowbray/The Alcuin Club, 1992.

Celebrating Common Prayer, Mowbray, 1992 (an Office Book from the Society of St Francis).

New Zealand Prayer Book, Collins, 1989 (this prayer book takes seriously both the modern and traditional cultures from which it comes; it is particularly helpful for modern collects).

Hannah Ward and Jennifer Wild, *Human Rites*, Mowbray, 1995 (this contains some radical liturgies, and some imaginative liturgies and ways of using the liturgy).

Ray Simpson, *Celtic Worship Through The Year*, Hodder & Stoughton, 1997.

Books offering advice on renewing the liturgy:

Michael Marshall, *Free To Worship*, Marshall Pickering, 1996.

John Leach, *Living Liturgy*, Kingsway, 1997.

John Gunstone, *Pentecost Comes to Church*, Darton, Longman & Todd, 1994.

Useful internet sites:

Modern Liturgy is a web site of an American Catholic publisher which offers some imaginative ways of celebrating the liturgy. It tends to be seasonally based.

[Web Site http://shell7.ba.best.com/~rpi/ml/ml.html]

Their address is: Resource Publications Inc., 160 E. Virginia St, San Jose, CA95112-5876, USA.

Greenbelt lists a number of alternative worship 'events', some of which lead to their own web sites.

[Web Site http://www.greenbelt.org.uk/altgrps/altg.html]

Robert Longman is a Roman Catholic site with basic, useful hints about the relationship between the Church's liturgy and the work of the Spirit.

[Web Site http://www.li.net/~rlongman/worship.html]

Worship in and for the world

The group in Britain which has led the way in comparable renewal of worship in recent years is the *Wild Goose Worship Group* of the Iona Community. They have published an extensive series of books, some of which contain songs written by John Bell (one of the leaders at San Antonio) and Graham Maule, make available musical items from around the world, and share liturgical elements and whole service out-lines. Write for the up-to-date list to: Wild Goose Publications, Iona Community, Unit 15, Six Harmony Row, Glasgow G51 3BA.

[Web Site http://www.iona.org.uk]

The single most useful publication of the World Council of Churches, Geneva, is probably the 184-page, ring-bound handbook *Worshipping*

45

Ecumenically, edited by Per Harling. It contains the full series of worship outlines and music from the San Antonio 1989 Conference and is available from: CCBI Publications Office, 35-41 Lower Marsh, London SE1 7RL, at £10.85 plus postage (ISBN 2-8254-1141-8).

Drawn to the Wonder was published by the Council for World Mission for its anniversary celebrations in 1995, and contains 50 hymns and songs from many different cultures and backgrounds, with singable English texts. Twenty of them are also available on cassette. Edited by the leader of Counterpoint, Maggie Hamilton, who was one of the leaders at Salvador, it is available from: CWM, Livingstone House, 11 Carteret St, London SW1H 9DL, for £ 4.50 plus postage (ISBN 0-905508-27-0).

World Praise was compiled by David Peacock and Geoffrey Weaver in 1993, originally for use by the Baptist World Alliance. However, it had in mind a wide use in many different and local settings. It contains 85 items, again from many different cultures and churches. It is published by: Marshall Pickering, HarperCollins Publishers, 77-85 Fulham Palace Road, Hammersmith, London W6 8JB, in both music (ISBN 0-551-04000-9) and words only (04001-7) editions.

3

Renewal through healing

Introduction

Healing is a subject long associated with spiritual renewal and evangelism. The evangelistic witness of the disciples following Pentecost regularly included acts of healing. Within days of the Pentecost experience, Peter and John find themselves engaged in the healing ministry towards a lame man outside the Jerusalem temple. This in turn led to his proclaiming the gospel to the astonished onlookers. In the infant Church the renewing work of the Holy Spirit, the proclamation of the gospel and acts of healing were closely interwoven. Throughout the history of the Church the healing ministry has always been closely associated with mission. In some cases this has led to Christian people being closely involved in the medical services and medical missions; in other cases it has led evangelists to include prayer for miraculous healing for the newly converted in their meetings. Sadly, these two expressions of the healing ministry have all too often been divided, but centres like Burrswood, the home for healing in Kent, model for us a holistic healing ministry in which medical help, prayer and anointing for healing with the laying-on of hands are used in harmony.

Many have found that an experience of healing has led them into a new and closer walk with God. Furthermore, those who engage in the ministry of healing have also often testified that it is for them an experience of personal renewal of faith. In this chapter we shall be looking at three stories of healing. The first two are stories of personal healing experienced by people engaged in medical work, and the third looks at the experience of healing in the context of an ethnic minority group. The stories alert us to the fact that today's society is greatly burdened by sickness – physical, emotional and social. It may be an inoperable cancer, an emotional wound that leads to recurring depression, or a profound sense of hurt due to rejection simply on the grounds of ethnic difference. Whatever the nature of the sickness, the Church in our day is thankfully rediscovering the tremendous resources for healing, and our three stories bring us very encouraging signs of this.

For the first story, I met with *Dr Gareth Tuckwell,* the Director of the Burrswood Christian Centre for Healthcare and Ministry. He offered me the story of *Dr Jane Thompson,* and with her permission I reproduce her testimony of personal healing. Through prayer with the laying-on of hands and a simple symbolic gesture, together with her courageous openness, the ministry of healing has led her to a deeper and more tender relationship with God. This has affected her work with her patients and her relationships in her family.

Revd Canon Anne Long has spent much of her life engaged in practising and teaching pastoral, listening and counselling skills. She has developed the 'Christian Listener' training programme which has now trained thousands of people throughout the British Isles and beyond in listening skills. She brings us the story of John, a consultant anaesthetist in an Oxford hospital. In some ways his healing need was similar to Jane's. The listening he received opened him up to healing and a new doorway to personal renewal. It also led him to a new experience of listening to God, which in turn led him into a new direction for his life.

Our third story is brought to us by *Deo Meghan,* a member of the MERE Committee who, in our first discussions of this book, urged the inclusion of a healing story related to the ethnic minority groups. Deo is a Reader in the Diocese of Coventry and Diocesan Link Person and Convenor of the Diocesan Group for Black and Asian Concerns. He is a member of the Committee for Minority Ethnic Anglican Concerns and a registered mental nurse. He brings us the moving stories of Millie and Rafiq, who suffered the great hurt of being rejected by their fellow-Christians simply because of the colour of their skin. Their testimony challenges us to work for that social healing which our society so badly needs. For if we truly believe that in Christ there is 'neither Jew nor Greek, slave nor free, male nor female', then we will long for the healing Holy Spirit to purge all prejudice and discrimination from our hearts, and seek to bring the healing presence of Christ to the racial wounds in our society. Justice will inevitably bring healing and renewal.

1. **Personal healing**   *Jane Thompson*

The following story was delivered at Fleet Baptist Church as part of the introduction to a service of healing in December 1997.

Some of you may have been at a service a little while ago when I read part of *The Pilgrim's Progress*, the story of Pilgrim letting go his burden at the foot of the cross. You may not have been aware that I too had been feeling that I was carrying a huge burden that I wanted to leave at the foot of the cross but somehow had been unable to let it go. We are told that Pilgrim's burden was his sin. For me, although I am aware of my sin, I did not feel that my burden was sin, but I could not see what it was. This burden was affecting my relationships with my family and friends; it was affecting my work, and there were times when I was very weepy and felt very dark. I found fulfilling all that I felt was expected of me was becoming too much to cope with.

I recently took the opportunity of spending a week on a doctors' residential updating refresher course at Burrswood, which is a Christian centre for healing. There is a hospital and a conference centre on site, with chapels, chaplains and counsellors, and I decided while I was there to claim some time for myself and see if I could find peace and healing for me.

I spent time with a counsellor who listened to my story, which I shared with her. I told her of my constant striving to achieve, my feeling that my best was never good enough, that I would never get things right and therefore the constant reminder that I was a failure. You may have looked at me and seen someone who had achieved a great deal – career, family, success, someone who was doing well – but those closest to me often saw sadness, tears, the lack of peace, and they tried to help me with this burden. I shared with the counsellor some of my memories and particularly sentences that had been said, which I heard repeating constantly in my head, that emphasized my feelings of failure.

As some of you may know, I came from a very academic background where achieving was very important. My three elder brothers went to Cambridge University, two of them have Ph.D.s and I thought that was what my parents wanted me to do too. I had a very happy childhood but I felt that the most important thing in life was not only to do my best but, if I was to gain my parents' approval, to be better than everyone else. I would not be where I am now without that upbringing and I am very grateful that I was encouraged to achieve my full potential in all areas of my life – music, sport, and in my training to be a doctor. But I lived with the nagging burden that my best was never good enough. I was always being encouraged to do better. I once got 100 per cent in a Scripture exam but was not praised because there were five people who had got 100 per cent and I had not got the gold medal! Because my best was not good enough I constantly failed. Even after working really hard at my medical training at London University for seven years, I was intro-duced to neighbours of my parents as 'This is my daughter, Jane. She is a doctor, but not a proper doctor – she has not got a Ph.D.'.

The counsellor suggested to me that my burden was the expectations that I and others had put on me. She suggested that I should meet with her and the chaplain in a small chapel to pray for healing and to leave my burden at the foot of the cross.

Later in the week I had nearly an hour free before I was due to meet with the counsellor and the chaplain and I sat on my own in the chapel. In the quietness I realized that not only had my burden been getting in the way of relationships with my family, but also, more importantly, of my relationship with God and this was threatening my inner peace.

I was able to share this with the chaplain and counsellor when we met together. I had no problem accepting the fatherhood of God: the model I had in my own parents was good and kind and my physical needs had been provided for, but the chaplain pointed out that as a daughter of God I was striving to achieve God's approval. I was carrying this huge burden of failure, of never being good enough, and the need to do more and to be better. The burden was still heavy and the lack of inner peace was a great sadness – the tears were never far away.

In his prayers the chaplain asked that I might be delivered from the words that had made such a deep impression, that I might be released from the need to keep striving, accept God's unconditional love and grace and realize that I was of value not for what I did and what I achieved but for who I am, a daughter of God and precious in his sight.

Following that prayer, I found that the burden was beginning to ease. In the tiny little chapel where we were meeting, there was an altar with a small cross carrying the body of Jesus, and at the foot of the cross there was a crown of thorns. The chaplain suggested that it might be helpful for me to gather up my damp tissues, my burden of striving, and leave them at the foot of the cross. I found the symbolism of that very powerful. It was some time before I could do it, but I did and, like Pilgrim, I came away from the cross knowing in my heart that God's love really is unconditional and I was free from the burden I had been carrying for so long.

That was the start to finding an inner peace that had seemed to be out of my reach. Since I have been back I haven't needed the tissues. I have found a new peace in my relationship with my mother. I have found that I can come alongside some of my heartsick patients, those I had previously found it difficult to love, in a totally different way, and relationships at work which had not been easy have been transformed as my attitude has changed. I am still the same person. I am sure that there will be times when I may get overwhelmed again and I may still do a lot of things – I shall still enjoy being the first away at the traffic lights – but I do not feel the same burden. I can choose to do, not because I ought to, striving to gain approval, but out of a greater desire to love and value others in the same way that I know I am loved and valued by God.

It has been awesome to experience God's healing hand in my relationships, in my work at the surgery and in my life, but more than that, to experience the sense of peace that healing has brought.

God does not promise to magic away pain and suffering, but we read that he is a God of compassion who has engraved us on the palms of his hands, desiring that we should be whole. I believe he is with us in our suffering and, as we know, Jesus endured more than we shall ever be asked to endure: 'Surely he has borne our infirmities and carried our diseases' (Isaiah 53.4).

2.   Healing through listening   *Anne Long*

Dietrich Bonhoeffer wrote:

> The first service that one owes to others in fellowship consists in listening to them. Just as love of God begins with listening to his word, so the beginning of love for the brethren is learning to listen to them. Listening, then, is part of loving service.

Not surprisingly, many move into a ministry of Christian listening through discovering that they themselves have personal needs to be listened to and heard. It is often through our own wounds being healed that God then uses us as wounded healers to others. Christ meets us at our own point of need, then sends us out to minister to those who hurt. That is how it was for *John*. John was, until recently, a consultant anaesthetist in the Oxford hospitals, specializing in neuro-surgery. In 1990 he was ordained priest in the Anglican Church and now, having retired from medicine, he works as a non-stipendiary minister with the Wheatley group of parishes in the Oxford diocese. He is also a Christian Listener tutor, as is his wife Pam, and they have three adult children. John tells his story.

I am now 63 years old and have been a Christian for half that time. My conversion was as dramatic as it was traumatic. After the death of my first wife, when I was in the depths of despair and grief, I met Jesus in person in the middle of the night in a hospital chapel. I was directed to meet a priest who listened to my story, said very little, but assured me of the reality of my 'religious experience'. He lent me a book, *The Cloud of Unknowing*, and sent me on my way to continue discovering God. And I did! That priest listened well.

In 1990 I was ordained as a priest in the Anglican Church and started to get very busy and involved in many things. I did not, however, feel affirmed by the church which had supported my training as a non-stipendiary minister. I realize now that, coming from a broken home, I had a number of patterns of behaviour which were to do with approval addiction. If I achieve then I will be affirmed and loved . . . maybe God will also love me! The outcome of all this was that I became busier and busier in St Aldate's Church because, in my confused longing for approval, I wanted them to see me as fulfilling a priestly role (whatever that might mean). So I became involved in leading the prayer ministry team, co-ordinating counselling and Christian Listeners. On top of this I was also mission co-ordinator for my church and helping with missions in other churches. At the same time as all this, I was working full time in the NHS as a consultant anaesthetist.

During one mission week I was asked to lead a workshop on stress management for Christians. I said 'Of course'. As I prepared, I realized that I myself had all the symptoms of burn-out. I cancelled the workshop.

Around this time (1992) my own interest and involvement in Christian Listeners was growing. Following a successful day workshop that I had arranged for our church, I was invited to train as a Christian Listener tutor. Realizing how much into overload I was, and feeling desperately in need of being listened to, I wrote to one of the CL staff and asked if we could meet. I needed someone whom I trusted and who was not part of the Oxford scene. To confess my problems there felt too much like failure. We met for half an hour over lunch at a Christian Listener tutors' meeting in Reading.

As I talked, my listener said little, although I realize now that I was allowed to explore how I was feeling and get in touch with some really painful rejections. I was not given any advice but the result was that I began to gain insight and understanding into what was happening to me. It was the start of a healing process which allowed me to give the Lord permission to come in again and show me new ways of living. It was that experience of someone listening to me and somehow listening to God for me that not only led me to a place of peace and restoration but showed me something of what God was preparing for me to do. Through that experience I learnt about 'hardening of the oughteries', trying to do all that was expected of me, rather than being 'just good enough'. I realized over the months that followed and through several single-day retreats (the desire for which seemed to have come out of that time of listening) that I was loved by God. I did not have to earn his love, even though I was part of a busy, goal-oriented church and profession. This was a mega discovery!

I next came into contact with my own needs when I allowed myself to listen to God through Scripture. This was something I had learnt a little about on the Christian Listener courses. Indeed, I had taught it to others. On a half-day retreat I was asked to sit in the wonderful garden of Highmoor Hall near Reading, look at Scripture and simply listen to God. At this time I was struggling with guidance. What was God calling me to and what should I do with the remaining five years of my medical work? The passage I looked at was from Mark 10, the account of Jesus healing the blind man. As I sat and read and prayed, a verse sprang out of the page. 'The crowd turned to the blind man and said, "Get up. Cheer up. He's calling you"' (v. 49). I got up, went home, wrote 12 letters of resignation and took early retirement from my medical life. I was given certainty and peace in that decision. I was then invited to train as an Ignatian spiritual director, paid for by Oxford Diocese, and moved into the quiet life of a part-time unpaid country parson. This gave me a flexible job description which allowed for work with the Acorn Trust and in spiritual direction.

Recently I found myself feeling very stressed again! I happened to be teaching a CL course with two colleagues. I agreed to be listened to by one of my colleagues whilst the group observed the listening process. I decided to explore how I felt as a father to my daughter, Juliet, who was preparing to go to Malawi for eight months with the Right Hand Trust, a small Anglican mission organization. As I talked I felt despair and anxiety. I suddenly got in touch with some dreadful anger both with God and with my wife. She had suggested in a light-hearted way that, as we might be in South Africa with a Christian Listeners Team at the same time as Juliet was in Malawi, we could go and see her. As I explored this and was invited to say more, I realized that I was in a really bad way, full of uncertainty and worry about my own safety and security in going to South Africa with Acorn. To think of going to Malawi as well was intolerable! It was irrational, and I was the little boy again who had been evacuated in the war never to be reunited with my broken home and family. I knew that I had further work to do with some of these feelings if I was to move forward. We ended the session with prayer for healing and peace.

Three days later I was at Burrswood and at breakfast I talked about Malawi and mentioned South Africa as well. One of the other doctors who was there shared her positive experiences in Malawi and then said 'Why don't you go to Malawi as well?' This time I felt peaceful at that suggestion. I searched inside for any other feelings. There were none. It was not just the catharsis of having spoken out and got in touch with feelings the previous week. There was no reason not to feel them again as, humanly, nothing had changed. I believe the Lord had heard me as well as the listener, and he had answered prayer, met my need and brought healing through that listening experience.

For me, each of these three experiences has been important and life-changing and has come about as a result of prayerful and faithful listening. I write this as my personal experience of the way in which Christ has met me at my point of need, healed me and brought clarification where before there was confusion, and feelings I never realized I had could be safely expressed.

For John, being listened to at certain crucial times in his adult life opened a door through which God met him at his point of need, bringing him clarification, healing, peace and a fresh encounter with Christ. God has also given John a growing ministry of listening to and training others. He has led Christian Listener courses for Oxford students and also for doctors. He and Pam lead courses for church groups and in March 1998 they went as part of a training team to teach Christian Listening in South Africa.

3.   Healing in a minority ethnic community *Deo Meghan*

For centuries people of different races, cultures and beliefs have been coming to England, but this became more evident in the forties, fifties and sixties. They came from the African, Asian and American continents as well as from the West Indian islands. Many will remember the *Empire Windrush*, which brought nearly 500 Jamaicans to the English shore in the summer of 1948. They brought with them a rich ethnic diversity of cultures, gifts, new skills and a range of wide experiences.

Many who came from the continents and the Caribbean islands were devout Christians and were brought up in the high church Anglican tradition. Yet when they tried to worship in the Anglican Church, which they regarded as their Mother Church, they were met with coldness. They were 'frozen' out. They faced rejection and alienation, and were marginalized and treated as if they were second-class citizens. Their pleas fell on deaf ears. They were not heard and had no voice. The difference in their colour and the way they spoke were not tolerated. In some cases they could stay in the church as long as they didn't do anything funny or behave in an inappropriate way. They felt humiliated and hurt. All they wanted was to be made welcome in the Anglican Church but only a few managed to find a home there; most drifted and joined the 'Black-led' churches where they felt a sense of belonging.

I first met *Millie* about ten years ago when she visited my parish church. She was born in Jamaica where she spent most of her childhood years worshipping in an Anglican church. She arrived in England in 1958 at the age of 18 and came to live with her sister in Coventry. At that time there were a large number of Asians and a few black people from the West Indies living in Coventry. But the number was increasing all the time as more black and Asian people were attracted to Coventry by the increasing prospect of employment. Millie soon found work in one of the local factories and was eager to attend church.

On the first available Sunday she decided to make her first visit to her local Anglican church. Millie spoke to me boldly, but with some sadness in her voice as she vividly recalled that first visit to the church. She said:

> I felt rather strange and unsure of what to expect, a
> little apprehensive and somewhat threatened being
> surrounded by so many white people staring at me.
> It was something which I wasn't used to especially
> when I looked back to my church days in Jamaica. I
> remember clearly that no one welcomed me on that
> first day in church but instead they all sat away from
> me. No one spoke to me or offered to help me in fol-
> lowing the service which I wasn't familiar with. I felt
> that people were deliberately avoiding me. I was very
> hurt.

Millie couldn't understand why no one whom she regarded as Christian
would say 'Hello' or 'Good morning' to her. To Millie this is just common
politeness, whether you know the person or not. Her worst fear – that
she was deliberately ignored because of her colour – was realized at the
end of the service when the priest approached her and told her, 'Don't
come here again, your presence is upsetting the congregation.' Millie
recalled: 'That was the worst day of my life.' She rushed home to her sister with her eyes filled with tears and could hardly find the words to tell
her how she had been treated in church. She asked herself, 'How can
Christians behave like this?' For the next fifteen years Millie carried that
hurt in her soul because she could not find the courage and confidence
to go back to church. During that time Millie married and had two children.

Healing for Millie began in 1974 when she moved to her own house in
a neighbouring parish. Her desire to go to church had never ceased but
she could not find the courage to do so. I believe that Millie could not
face another rejection in church. However, she did make some enquiries
about her local church and received an invitation from one of its members to come along to a Sunday service. On her first visit to her new local
church she was made welcome and valued for the person she was. She
said, 'I immediately felt a sense of belonging and the people there made
a fuss of me.' The white priest at this Anglican church was married to a
West Indian/Guyanese woman and therefore was aware of how black
people were treated and also understood their culture. Today, after 24

years, Millie is still happily worshipping regularly at this church where she has made many friends and valuable contributions to the life of the church, as well as serving as a PCC member and churchwarden for many years. She boasts that she has hardly missed Sunday worship during that time. Millie said: 'I am content and have found a home here in this beautiful church. I long to forgive those who hurt me and caused me to miss going to church all those years.'

I first met *Rafiq* at a vocation day in 1986 when we were both exploring the Reader ministry at the Diocesan Retreat House in Coventry. Rafiq is a 49-year-old Asian Christian and is married with two children. He was born and raised in an Anglican family in Punjab, India, where he was ordained as a deacon. In 1968, at the age of twenty, he came to England and settled with relatives in Coventry. Although Rafiq met with some problems at the beginning, he was determined not to let anything interfere with his regular worship at his local Anglican church. His ordination as a deacon in India was not recognized by his parish priest but he was allowed to preach from time to time, read the lessons and serve as a Eucharist Assistant.

In 1985 he offered himself for the ordained ministry but was told that he should first explore the possibility of the Reader ministry. At first he was encouraged by his priest to explore his call to the ministry. He was asked to do further courses, including a course at the Selly Oak Colleges. Everything he was asked to do, he did in the certain hope and confidence that he would be assisted and supported in pursuing his call to the ministry. Rafiq said:

> I spent three years preparing myself with my priest's encouragement but when I asked him to support my application for the Reader training, he simply refused, saying that I wasn't a suitable candidate. I was devastated and hurt at hearing this. All my hopes seemed to be dashed, as if I was being taken for a ride and all the study was a waste of time.

This was very painful for him and the feeling of rejection and hurt stayed with him for many years. For Rafiq, the healing began when he was counselled by a bishop's black adviser from Birmingham Diocese. During this time he was still attending the parish church where he was rejected. One day in 1996, as he was driving past another parish church, he noticed the name of an Asian priest. After a few years without a minority ethnic priest, in November 1995 Coventry Diocese appointed an Asian priest, Revd Supriyo Mukhergee, who is also the Diocesan Community Relations Adviser. Rafiq recalled saying, 'God sends him for me'. He immediately booked an appointment with him and by the following Sunday began to attend and worship there, where he is very happy. I am pleased to say that under the guidance of this new Asian priest, without any further training, Rafiq has recently been licensed as a Reader. I reminded him that all those studies were not a waste of time. This is indeed a happy ending for Rafiq; in his own words, 'A dream come true. God has heard my prayers and as a fulfilled person, I will now serve Him to the end.'

Black people who profess the Christian faith are Christians whether their ethnic origins lie in Africa, Asia, the Americas or the Caribbean islands. They belong to the Anglican Church and need to be welcomed and included, affirmed and listened to, recognized and valued for what they are and not excluded and alienated because of the colour of their skin. Although black Christians suffered the pain of rejection in silence for many decades, the dawn of renewal and healing began with the publication of the *Faith in the City* report in 1985, which brought the problems to the attention of the whole nation and Church. The subsequent publication of the *Seeds of Hope* report in 1991 showed the extent of racism in the Church of England, and the *Passing Winter* report in 1996 shows the progress and good practices which the Anglican Church has taken on board to raise awareness of racism and educate the people in the congregations about ethnic diversity and the strength of its cultural inheritance present in the gifts and contributions from its Black and Asian Christians. The July celebration in 1994 at York made a tremendous impact on the whole Church, and the ongoing work of the Committee for Minority Ethnic Anglican Concerns is constantly at the forefront of renewal and healing as we strive for unity and justice for all.

For reflection

1.   Which of the three healing stories attracts you most?

2.   What particular feature of the healing appeals to you?

3.   Are there practical steps you can take to explore it further?

4.   If there is a healing ministry in your church, are you happy with it? Is there any way you would like to see it develop?

5.   As you consider the first two stories, are there areas of your own personal history that you would like to offer for healing prayer?

6.   How do you react to Deo's stories about Millie and Rafiq? Are there any areas of prejudice that you would like to offer to God for healing? Prayerfully consider if there are ways you can help to heal the divides between races.

Resources

Personal healing

Burrswood Christian Centre for Healthcare and Ministry offers help with rehabilitation following surgery, emotionally triggered dis-ease and stress, acute medical illness, respite for those with disabilities, and palliative and terminal care. Write to: Burrswood, Groombridge,Tunbridge Wells, Kent TN3 9PY (Tel: 01892 863637).

Wholeness magazine provides news and reflection on the ministry of healing. Write to: *Healing and Wholeness*, Broadway House, The Broadway, Crowborough, Sussex TN6 1HQ.

The Church's Council for Health and Healing Write to: St Marylebone Parish Church, Marylebone Road, London NW1 5LT (Tel: 0171 486 9611).

The Guild of Health Write to: The Guild of Health, Edward Wilson House, 26 Queen Anne Street, London W1M 9LB (Tel: 0171 580 2492).

The Guild of St.Raphael Write to: The Guild of St Raphael, The Vicarage, Skirwith, Penrith CA10 1RQ (Tel: 01768 88663).

Healing through listening

The Acorn Christian Healing Trust was founded in 1983 by Bishop Morris and Anne Maddocks. The vision God gave them was of a church and nation renewed in the service of Christ the Healer. Acorn seeks to promote co-operation between the Church and medicine, provide teaching and training resources and develop all aspects of the Christian healing ministry. One of the Acorn projects is *Christian Listeners*. After training, Listeners work in a wide variety of contexts, both within churches and cathedrals and in outreach into the local community – hospitals, hospices, the social services, prisons, schools. Christian Listener training is also used by some dioceses in their lay training courses, such as the Bishop's Foundation Course in Chester and the Pastoral Assistants' course in Rochester. All the courses include the three threads of listening to people, to God and to ourselves. People are not equipped to become counsellors, which these days requires a professional training, but to be responsible listeners, working under supervision. For further information about Christian Listeners write to: The Acorn Christian Healing Trust, Whitehill Chase, High Street, Bordon, Hants GU35 0AP (Tel: 01420 478121; Fax: 01420 478122).

Healing in a minority ethnic community

For further information on the issues raised in this essay, write to: The Secretary, Committee for Minority Ethnic Anglican Concerns, Church House, Great Smith Street, London SW1P 3NZ (Tel: 0171 222 9011).

4

Renewal through communities

Introduction

Arguably the first renewal movement in the Church was the emergence
of the desert fathers and mothers in Egypt which began with St Antony
towards the end of the third century. With the conversion of the Roman
Emperor to Christianity, the Church lost much of the spiritual fire that
had kept it burning bright in the days of persecution. Thousands of men
and women felt called to go into the wilderness to fast and pray and be
witnesses to spiritual life and power in a church that was becoming
increasingly nominal. Whilst some, like Antony, preferred to live alone,
others sought to express this life in community. Thus, the first expressions of monastic life were born with disciplines of worship, prayer and
witness.

Ever since then the monastic witness has played a vital part in the life of
the Church. In recent years we have witnessed a resurgence of interest
in the disciplines of retreats and spiritual direction, and this has led
thousands to make connections with the various convents and monasteries in the Church which offer spiritual guidance and support. We
have also seen during this century the emergence of new communities
which have no direct relation to the established communities such as the
Benedictines or Franciscans, but which are none the less centres of
Christian hospitality and spiritual renewal. Whether these communities
are ancient or modern, formal or informal, they are proving to be a vital
resource for renewal. Not only is the shared life of such communities an
influence for renewal, but often the place where the community lives is
experienced as a place of peace, holiness and healing. The little island of
Iona is a clear example of this, steeped as it is in rich Christian history.
Lee Abbey is another, set in its dramatic North Devon landscape of

rolling hills and rocky headland. The quiet chapel in an inner-city convent also holds its own striking beauty and becomes a place of renewal. Such places are experienced by many as holy ground and, as such, as meeting places with God.

In this chapter I share my own story of encounters with the more traditional religious communities, and so represent the many who are discovering such places as rich resources for renewal. We also include stories from the two modern communities already mentioned. *Revd Peter Millar* is a minister of the Church of Scotland and Warden of Iona Abbey. He worked in the Church of South India for many years. He and his wife Dorothy, a former consultant pathologist, have written on a wide variety of subjects and Peter's most recent book is *A Pilgrim Guide to Iona*. The Iona Community, founded in 1938, has been a focus of renewal since its beginnings in the inner-city area of Govan in Glasgow. Its founder, George MacLeod (later the Very Revd Lord MacLeod of Fuinary), and the early members were determined to link the message of the gospel with the hopes and struggles of ordinary people. In the last 60 years, the community has been committed to seeking new ways of living the gospel in today's world. The island has become the focus of pilgrimage for thousands of people.

The third story in this chapter is by *Mandy Wright*, who writes of her visit to Lee Abbey. This is a story of one person's experience of community living and of how God has used that community to heal, renew and transform both the individual and the Church. Lee Abbey is a large country house standing in 280 acres of stunning North Devon coastal scenery. It houses a permanent community of between 70 and 80 people, drawn from all backgrounds, denominations and countries. At the time of writing, the community included representatives from as far afield as Australia, America, Africa, Singapore and several Eastern European countries. Denominations ranged from Roman Catholic, Methodist, Anglican and Lutheran to Free Church and house church representatives. Lee Abbey is a holiday, retreat and conference centre and the community exists to minister to the 7,000 guests who pass through its doors each year.

The three expressions of community described in this chapter are gatherings of committed people who seek to live a shared life, and it is that expression of shared life which is proving to be such a keen influence of spiritual renewal for those who visit.

1. The convent and monastery *Michael Mitton*

During my teens I found myself being influenced by evangelical spirituality more than any other. By the time I was at university studying theology, I was well involved in the University Christian Union and, on being accepted to train for the ordained ministry, it was natural for me to head for an evangelical training college. I thus found myself completing my training at St John's College, Nottingham. It was here that I discovered that there were dimensions of my Christian life which could not be expressed in the culture of evangelicalism. I longed for stillness, sometimes solitude, and I explored the catholic tradition. I was fortunate at St John's to be taught by staff who were also on a similar journey, and I discovered that they made regular visits to convents and monasteries for personal retreats.

I had never in all my life been inside such a place! I certainly had no idea how you would go about visiting one. But at this time my father had been invited to bring his business skills to bear on a declining convent in Buckinghamshire which was seeking to move from its huge Victorian home to a smaller dwelling. The Mother Superior, on hearing I was an ordinand, invited me to use the guest room for a private retreat. So it was that I found myself nervously entering this vast convent building one warm July day for an overnight stay. I was welcomed by a kind sister and led up a long winding staircase to a room in the tower. I was shown the chapel, and the place where I would have my meals. The rest, as Hamlet said, was silence. At first, it was very unnerving being in this large place, not knowing a soul, and every now and again seeing silent figures stealthily slipping down corridors. I could not find my way round the complexity of the office books in the chapel, and if I did try and sing during the services, my male voice sounded far too conspicuous. But despite these little insecurities, I found a most welcome tranquillity. I felt enfolded in prayer. The spiritual dedication of this small group of largely elderly Benedictine sisters provided a platform from which I could explore God and the various issues of my life at that time, with new clarity and energy. I returned from my 24-hour retreat certainly refreshed and renewed.

My next encounter with a religious community was my pre-ordination retreat at Nashdom Abbey. This time it was a male order that cared for me. Still a huge building, still unfamiliar liturgies, still anxieties about going where I shouldn't or breaking some rule or other, yet again I met the tranquillity. And this time it was so welcome, amidst all my pre-ordination nerves. I developed the rhythm of walks in the warm beechwoods, times of reading and times of prayer. Once ordained and a curate in the Oxford Diocese, I continued my discipline of a regular annual retreat at the convent, which had now moved to smaller premises. My preference was not to go on a conducted retreat. I would now go for a couple of days and work out a routine of prayer, reading, walking and resting. These became lifelines and special times of discovering God in a new way.

When I moved to the Worcester Diocese I soon discovered the Community of the Holy Name at Malvern. This beautiful convent had one other great attraction for me – the Malvern Hills! My annual retreat here became a spiritual oasis. Times of stillness in the chapel would be matched by long walks up the hills. After the pressures of a busy parish life, these were times when it felt as if my spirit was given room to breathe. At first I still had to get used to the new routines and my unfamiliarity with the schedules of the religious life always threatened to get me into trouble. On my first visit, I decided to go for an evening walk to the hills, as I wanted to watch the sunset. However, I failed to discover that 9.00pm was lock-out at the convent! On my return all doors were firmly locked and bolted! Thankfully, I found an open window, but great was my anxiety on climbing through it lest I found myself somewhere I shouldn't be. Mercifully it was an innocuous room and I sped silently to my bedroom.

During my time in this diocese I also made friends with Brother Ramon, who was at the time guardian of Glasshampton Monastery. This was really my first chance of getting to know someone in the religious life. My friendship with Ramon has been very important to my spiritual journey, especially since he has been called to live as a hermit. His witness to solitude and stillness has been of great comfort to me in my life, which is usually too crowded and busy. I moved to Derby much the same time as the Community of the Holy Name moved there and I have much appreciated my visits to them.

I have now settled into a routine of taking an annual three-day retreat at Glasshampton Monastery. My retreat last year opened a new door of exploration as I found myself led into reading about some of the medieval Christian mystics. The rhythm of reading, walking and prayer was a deeply renewing experience for me, and began a whole new rediscovery of the love of God that has had a great impact on me.

I think I know myself well enough now to recognize the environment which suits me best for a retreat that will be a renewing experience for me. The important components are plenty of time and space, silent meals, solitude, regular worship, sleep, reading and long walks. The convents and monasteries that I have visited have been immensely welcoming and have given me the freedom I needed for my retreat. Other people prefer more company on their retreats and find too much solitude difficult. They will prefer going on retreat with groups. Others may go on their own, but on a conducted retreat, with regular meetings with a member of the community for guidance. Some orders, for example the Franciscans, offer a Third Order, which enables people to take on a rule of life with regular spiritual direction and thereby form a much closer link with the community. Monasteries and convents have always been an integral source of inspiration for prayer, renewal and mission, and in the current culture and climate of our time their contribution is becoming even more vital.

2.   The Iona Community   *Peter Millar*

As we move into a new century, the island of Iona, spiritual home to the ecumenical Iona Community, remains a place of pilgrimage from every corner of the world. In 1997, around 200,000 people landed on its sacred shores – pilgrims and seekers all. The community today is a movement of around 200 Members, 1800 Associate Members and about 1600 Friends. The Members – women and men from many backgrounds and denominations, most living in Britain, but some overseas – are committed to a rule of daily prayer and Bible reading, sharing and accounting for their use of time and money, regular meeting and action for peace and justice.

Apart from its three centres on Iona and Mull, the community has a mainland base in Glasgow where it also supports work with young people, the Wild Goose Resource and Worship Groups, a bi-monthly magazine (*Coracle*), and a publishing house (Wild Goose Publications).

The ministry on the island of Iona is sustained by a resident group of around 25 people, along with 150 seasonal volunteers who come from around the world. About 100 guests stay at the centres each week between March and October, sharing completely in the 'common life' of meals, worship, chores, reflection and social activities. The morning, midday and evening services are led by members of the resident group, volunteers and guests and reflect the central concerns of the community – welcome, justice and peace, healing, pilgrimage, commitment, celebration and mission. The community also has an extensive ministry on Iona to hundreds of pilgrim groups, day visitors and the many others who stay on the island for shorter or longer periods.

Many of those who come to stay in the community's centres on Iona are experiencing inner journeys of great pain. This story is about *Val*. She was brought up on a large Glasgow housing estate, and poverty, unemployment, abuse, drugs and broken relationships have been her constant companions these last twenty years. I see Val as a truly contemporary person, because her life mirrors much of the violence and abandonment of our times. Val came to stay at the community's MacLeod Centre in 1966 with a group of folk who were trying to kick drugs. She was both vulnerable and wounded, and like many who come to Iona, wanted to share her story. It was not long before she discovered listening ears and a gentle, encompassing compassion. She saw that she was accepted as she was – a broken but also strong woman.

On Iona, as we share the common life, new inner journeys often begin around the kitchen sink or in the craft room. She made friends in both places, and also found, much to her astonishment, that she could make beautiful clay figures which were appreciated by others. We all too easily clothe the gospel in totally unnecessary language, but in places like Iona we are forced (sometimes, it seems, 24 hours a day) by the Vals of our world to announce the Good News within the laughter, anger, tears and misunderstandings of the common life. No easy task! We can never be six feet above criticism in a pulpit – which is why we learn so much about God from folk like Val and countless others. For me, they reveal great chunks of the gospel just by the very nature of their brokenness, humour, courage and pain. In a situation where work and prayer interweave, guests like Val often seem to feel at home relatively quickly. She herself had no links at all with institutional Christianity, and seemed helped by the fact that others on Iona were in the same position. At one level, Iona is steeped in centuries of religious tradition, while at another there is a lightness and freshness about its expression of Christian faith. This has something (or all) to do with the fact that the ups and downs of daily living are never distant from our prayers and silences and songs. Nothing is insignificant: washing the dishes together reflects our life of prayer and worship just as much as our hymns in the abbey church. The whole of life is holy – a basic truth held by both our Columban and Benedictine forebears on Iona.

I would say without hesitation that the journey into Christ for a friend like Val can only come about if we (who often wrongly imagine that we alone possess biblical truth) are willing to listen and enter into solidarity with the person beside us. This does not mean that we become tongue-tied in speaking about Jesus, but can we do that with integrity, without first moving into a relationship of acceptance? Val is much more than a drug addict: she is a person held in God's hands. And she is accepted by him in her vulnerability.

From her first day on Iona, Val loved the gentle beauty of the abbey church, illumined, as it often is, by the extraordinary light of a Hebridean sky. She keeps telling me that she could sit for hours in the church. And often, late in the evening, she goes to the South Aisle, which is set aside as a prayer chapel, and watches the candles glow against the rough-hewn walls while listening to the restless tides in the Sound of Iona beyond.

Occasionally when Val is staying at the Abbey, I see her sharing her story with more 'orthodox' guests. She never tells it with arrogance or false humility, just as a matter of fact. Her language can often be rich in imagery, but her humanity is what captures her hearers. During her second visit to Iona, she asked me for a Bible, and painstakingly and slowly began to read Mark's Gospel. Soon she was asking me tremendously exciting questions about Jesus and his healing power. For me this is theology on the hoof – brilliant in its vitality and challenge!

I vividly remember a volunteer from Guatemala laying his hands on Val's head during the Tuesday evening service of prayers for healing. Along with the rest of the large congregation, Mario repeated the powerful prayer we often use on Iona: 'Spirit of the living God, present with us now, enter you, body, mind and spirit, and heal you of all that harms you, in Jesus' name.' Looking at Val's tearstained face as she listened to the prayer, I knew that the Spirit of the healing Christ was flowing through her mind and body. Val knew that too – not in the same way as I did, but in her own way (which was perhaps at a much deeper level than my own experience!). It was a moment of new life, of resurrection. An open heart receiving Christ.

Sometimes we speak of 'renewal' in much too glib a way – as if we can define it according to our own presuppositions. Val has revealed to me both the depth and the mystery of the gospel's power and the many-faceted ways in which Christ touches lives. I am certain that Val has come into contact with God's forgiving, energizing and healing grace in a very deep way, but exactly how that has happened in her life is not easy to analyse. Thank goodness! The translator, J. B. Phillips, was right when he said that for most of the time our God is too small.

Val's story continues to unfold in many dimensions. Her battle with drugs continues and her lack of confidence often overwhelms her completely. Yet she has experienced a new strength within and is determined to trust in God's guidance in a way which humbles me greatly. As the chorus says, she is not sure about what the future will hold, but she certainly knows the One who will hold it. That must be faith in Christ; and not least because it is so incredibly real. Back home in Glasgow, Val has not been in contact with a local church, although she has visited the homes of some Iona Community members and has found these visits extremely supportive. This coming Easter, Val and her boyfriend, who is also trying to kick drugs, will return to the abbey. They will share, with hundreds of others, the events of Holy Week and I have no doubt in my mind that for Val and Derek, who has also stayed at the abbey, these will be special days. Both of them are open to the accepting love of Jesus and the power of prayer in a remarkable way. Perhaps it is because they have entered so profoundly into their own failures that they experience so powerfully the radiance of Christ's light. When I see them bowed in prayer, I am reminded of a verse of a song from the Iona Community:

> Feel for the lives by life confused,
> Riddled with doubt, in loving abused;
> Feel for the lonely heart, conscious of sin,
> Which longs to be pure but fears to begin.

Val *has* begun, despite all her fears and hesitations. Like many of the wounded people in the gospels, she has experienced Jesus with her on the road of life. There will be innumerable hurdles ahead, but in a way which I am reluctant to define or even describe, Val, through poverty, abuse and humiliation, has found her Lord and been renewed. I can only give thanks to God that I have been privileged to share a small part of her incredible journey.

The Vals and Dereks who come to Iona carry in their lives an enormous challenge for our churches. They raise many questions. Are the values which permeate so many of our churches not simply mirroring the society which folk like Val and Derek have found so empty? Of course we may not mirror the drug culture, but is there that depth of spirituality within our congregations which can enable us to walk *alongside* Val and Derek, rather than telling them how to behave? What kind of welcome do we show them? Are we willing, in a prayerful way, to *learn* from their lives and perhaps be transformed ourselves by entering into their vulnerability? What truth is Christ seeking to reveal to us through friends like Val? Is our own faith static, or do we see ourselves as on a pilgrimage in which there are often more questions than answers? Have we been honest enough to lay our own brokenness at the feet of Christ?

Christian renewal has many faces. We know from our ministry on Iona that the Holy Spirit is moving in amazing ways; in our technological Western societies, thousands upon thousands are seeking Christ's light and forgiveness. It is a moment of great possibility and challenge for the world Church. Yet it is also a moment for all of us who claim to be followers of Christ to walk in humility and prayerful awareness. On the pilgrim route beside us are many who are often described as marginalized: those on the edge of society. It is worth remembering that in God's upside down kingdom, it will be these same folk who lead us to the banquet.

3. The Lee Abbey Community   *Mandy Wright*

Lee Abbey has a threefold vision: to build community; to renew and serve the Church; and to be God's welcome to all who come to us. The concept of building community is one which currently occupies the minds of both the Church and the nation. We have found that, in order for our community to exist in a healthy way, it is necessary for each member to be open, known for who they really are, ready to forgive others and to keep short accounts with both God and each other, to accept others as they are, regardless of denomination, nationality or personality and, most importantly, to be open to being changed and changed again by the Holy Spirit. Our love for God is the glue binding us together and our vision of service to the Church is what keeps us moving on. The story shows how God, working through a community based on these principles, can transform lives.

I joined the Devon community in January 1996 and currently work on the estate team, caring for the animals and grounds. I am due to remain at Lee Abbey until the middle of 1998. This story is a personal account of a journey. This journey took me to the depths of despair and to the point where I almost lost my faith entirely, then through a period of two years in which miracles large and small were almost the order of the day and when, through a constant cycle of breaking and remoulding, I was transformed into the 'new creation' I am today. It is a story of how God, with our co-operation, can take any circumstances, however apparently negative, and use them for good. Mostly, however, it is a story of how God works when we live together in community. How he transforms us as individuals, how he can transform a community who are trying to live in the way Christ commanded us and how he can touch, transform and renew the people who come as guests within the community.

The journey of renewal began for me when I was 35 years old. I had been a Christian for four years. I belonged to an Anglican Church which, at the time, was going through a period of change from traditional Prayer Book services, low numbers and little involvement from the congregation, to a more welcoming church with a variety of services, and a place where people were starting to get to know each other and to care for one another. It was a difficult period of change in which the Holy Spirit was constantly prompting us to repentance, reconciliation and openness.

I had been a police officer for sixteen years and by 1995 I was in a position of authority in the criminal investigation department. This particular year turned out to be the hardest of my life. I had been working on a murder squad, which was physically, emotionally and spiritually very draining. At the beginning of the year I had formed a relationship with a married man and then in the March of that year, my father died. Shortly after this, my situation was such that I had to choose between the relationship with the man with whom I had fallen in love and God. I chose the relationship. I was still attending church, but at this time, it was a place where, when people asked how you were, they were only open to the reply 'I'm fine'. Because of this, I did not seek help from anyone.

Eventually things came to a head. The relationship broke down and I was left without the man, without God and without the respect of my family or work, both of whom had discovered what was going on. I was in despair and even seriously contemplated suicide. God then stepped in and reminded me of Lee Abbey. I had visited this Christian conference and holiday centre on several occasions in the previous two years and had been very attracted by the way the community related to each other and to those of us who visited. One of the chaplains had had a particular influence on me and my faith, so I decided to go there, really as a last hope and an escape from an intolerable situation.

I was there for ten days. On the first day there, standing on a path amid the stunning scenery of North Devon, I had a picture of God the father, 'hitching up his skirts' and coming running to meet me, his lost child. The Holy Spirit worked through the love and acceptance I found in the community (acceptance, despite the fact that some of them knew my history), and through them showed me the meaning of repentance and forgiveness. Through them, I regained my relationship with God and was strengthened sufficiently to return home and to resist re-forming the relationship with the man.

Through this contact with community, I realized how low I had sunk and how easily shaken my faith was, as well as how lonely I was, despite my work and church fellowship. I decided to take unpaid leave from the police and to apply to join the community for a period of time. My motives at the time were mostly selfish. I wanted to live in a place where I would be loved and accepted and where I could renew and strengthen my relationship with God, but the Lord had so much more in store for me.

I suppose I had imagined that living in a community of Christians would be like living in heaven: all my problems, fears and pain would disappear and I would just float along on a cloud of love. I was wrong! Having lived alone for 16 years, I found that learning to live, worship and work with 70 other people was not always the total joy I had expected! The hardest lesson I had to learn was how to remove the mask I had spent years fashioning for myself. It was a mask that had stood me in good stead in the police force and one that I could hide behind to avoid the risk of being hurt.

We take a promise in the community which reads as follows:

> Are you prepared to learn to live in fellowship, being open to be known for what we are, accepting one another in Christ and saying of others nothing that could not be said to them personally if love and wisdom required it?

There are many implications to this promise and most of them I found extremely difficult. I had such a lack of trust in people that I had to go through an almost constant process of breaking and remoulding for most of the first two years. I learnt that, although my relationship with God was the most important facet of my life, relationships with others were also vital and that those involved pain as well as joy. The Holy Spirit helped me by revealing areas in my past which hindered my forming good relationships and then, through prayer, healing those areas. He also showed me that I needed to explore the meaning of humility – plenty of scope for exploration when you are living so closely with others. It was through being humbled in various circumstances that I grew the most.

I saw such miracles whilst living at Lee Abbey. I saw church groups coming for a parish weekend, dry, stale and with no passion for moving forward. God would meet them through the community and they would return revitalized and on fire for God. I saw broken individuals who came for a week with no hope or expectation of change, being healed physically, emotionally and spiritually. Sometimes this was through the direct intervention of the Holy Spirit in a miraculous way, but more often it was through the experience of being enveloped in the love of God through the people around them. I saw such changes in people in the community. A person would arrive and it was such a joy and privilege to see them open up, grow, and be transformed like a beautiful flower through the Holy Spirit's work. I watched people who had come with no direction to their life, sort out their priorities with God and take off, sometimes in a totally new and exciting direction.

I had come to the community thinking it would be an eleven-month break from the police and a time of rest and refreshment before returning. However, our God is a God of surprises and within nine months I had resigned from the police and had then spent time listening to God for my next direction. Patience is also a virtue you learn in community. God eventually made his wishes for me clear and I am currently in the selection procedure for the ordained ministry. I know that this purpose for me would never have been worked out if it had not been for God using the Lee Abbey community. He had to take me to a place where I could learn to trust and feel safe and where I could not escape my own failings and weaknesses, in order to transform me and strengthen those gifts and skills I already had, as well as introduce me to some which I had no idea I possessed.

I believe that the concept of true community has a lot to offer the Church today. Our aim at Lee Abbey is to communicate Christ through relationships. We need to love each other in our churches and thereby offer something to the world that it is desperately seeking. We need to rediscover that we are all parts of the same body and that our differences are not as important as what we have in common. Renewal begins, I believe, with Christ's love being shown through people and this is what we need if people are once again to say, 'See how these Christians love one another.'

My personal spiritual renewal began with God rescuing me from an impossible situation, forgiving me my many sins and then putting me in a community where I could be broken and re-formed and where I could begin to become the person he designed me to be. My prayer is that every church becomes a place where this transforming work is possible and where people are loved back into life. I know this can happen because, as God is constantly reminding me, with him nothing is impossible.

For reflection

1. Which of the three communities described above attracts you most?

2. What particular feature of that community appeals to you?

3. Are there practical steps you can take to explore this aspect further?

4. Do you make a regular retreat? If not, is now the time for you to be exploring the possibility of making a retreat?

5. Have you visited a place like the island of Iona, which many experience as a holy place? Consider visiting some of the holy islands, shrines, abbey ruins, cathedrals, ancient churches, which have been visited by Christians over the centuries. Use it as an opportunity for meeting with God in a new way.

6. Thinking of Mandy's last comment ('My prayer is that every church becomes a place where this transforming work is possible and where people are loved back into life'), reflect on your own church. Is there anything you can do to help your church grow as such a place?

Resources

The convent and monastery

A useful resource, giving information about communities and retreats, is *Retreats* (formerly called *The Vision*). This is the annual publication of the National Retreat Association and gives information about monasteries, convents and other centres which provide retreats. There are also useful articles which give practical help on making a retreat.

The Iona Community

For information write to: The Iona Community, Pearce Institute, 840 Govan Road, Glasgow G51 3UU (Tel: 0141 445 4561; Fax: 0141 445 4295; web site: http://www.iona.org.uk).

Lee Abbey Community

For information or a brochure about Lee Abbey, please write to: The Lee Abbey Fellowship, Lynton, North Devon EX35 6JJ (Tel: 01598 752621). For additional information on the history and ministry of the fellowship, *The Lee Abbey Story* by Richard More is published by Eagle and available at Christian book shops.

The Lee Abbey fellowship has two other areas of ministry. At the International Students Club in London the community provides accommodation for people of all religions and nationalities and seeks to show Christian love to all by its service to the students. There are also three household communities in Blackburn, Aston and Bristol where small groups live within deprived areas and bring the concept of community to those among whom they live.

5

Renewal through large gatherings

Introduction

Even a cursory reading of the gospels tells us that there were frequent occasions in the earthly ministry of Jesus when he addressed very large crowds. Matthew tells us that 'great crowds' followed Jesus (e.g. Matthew 8.1, 13.2), and one such great crowd was of at least 5,000 men, which clearly means that the total number including women and children was a good deal higher. Although we also have many accounts of his wanting to get away from the crowds, there is no doubt that there were times when Jesus affirmed the large gathering. Though there is always the apparent danger of being lost in the crowd, the story of the healing of the woman with the haemorrhage (Luke 8.42b – 48) tells us that even the person trying to be hidden in a crowd is noticed by God.

Throughout the history of the Church, Christian people have expressed their life and witness corporately. Usually the corporate life is expressed in the context of the regular Sunday worship community that meets at church. But there have always been occasions for large crowds to gather. Sometimes these have been for pilgrimages of penance, like the great pilgrimages of the Middle Ages. On other occasions they have been quests for healing, such as the huge numbers that gather at Lourdes. There have also been large evangelistic rallies, like the meetings of the Wesleys in the eighteenth century and the evangelist Billy Graham in this century. For some, the vast numbers of people can be intimidating, but for many people these large gatherings give great opportunities for a renewal that affects their own Christian life, and often also the life of their church.

In this chapter we look at three very different large gatherings which are currently annual events. The first story is provided for us by *Fr Martin*

Warner, who is the Priest Administrator of Walsingham, a pilgrimage centre in Norfolk, five miles inland from the sea. This centre has a long history of devotion to Mary, the mother of Jesus. This devotion is centred on the annunciation, an event made vivid by the representation of the house in Nazareth where Mary lived. Martin introduces us to Walsingham, and then tells us about a 'gentle miracle' that happened to someone called Anna.

The second story is about *Spring Harvest.* This event takes place during the weeks around Easter at large holiday centres on the British coast. The event has grown from humble beginnings twenty years ago to become the biggest Christian celebration-cum-holiday in Europe, annually attracting around 70,000 people of all ages. *Graham Gilliland* tells the story of his first visit to Spring Harvest.

Our third story is about a summer event called *New Wine.* This is an annual summer conference for families and church groups held at the Bath and West Showground at Shepton Mallet, Somerset; 7,500 adults, young people and children gather for this week-long event in August, camping or caravanning and meeting in the various showground meeting halls and marquees. The event grew out of the ministry of Bishop David Pytches during his time as vicar of St. Andrew's, Chorleywood, Hertfordshire and was first held in 1989. *Karen Sherman* tells us her story of spiritual and emotional healing during her visit to this event.

The three large gatherings are different in style, focus and spirituality, yet they all offer opportunities for spiritual renewal and have proved themselves over the years to be rich resources for individual Christians and church groups.

1. Walsingham   *Martin Warner*

Of the limited range of hymns on which I grew up, 'To be a pilgrim' was one of the most memorable, and my mother's favourite. Its original context in Bunyan's *The Pilgrim's Progress* suggested that pilgrimage belonged to the realms of history and scriptural symbolism. Never did I imagine it might be the stuff of my daily life!

Pilgrimage to Walsingham in Norfolk certainly belongs to the realm of history. Its origins go back at least to the twelfth century, when a woman of noble birth and godly life received a vision in which she was asked to build a replica of Mary's house in Nazareth. At a time when the holy sites of Jesus' life on earth exercised a powerful influence over people's imagination, the opportunity to visit Nazareth in England was eagerly seized upon. No matter what excesses the reformers perceived in the development of pilgrimage throughout the medieval period, its origins are essentially scriptural. Abraham, the Old Testament figure of faith, is a pilgrim. The children of Israel are constituted as God's chosen nation through their pilgrimage experiences in the wilderness. Even political exile provides a context for the prophets to speak about a pilgrimage journey of return and restoration.

As a holy gathering place, Walsingham is first of all about *particularity* – of time, place and person. Secondly it is about *hiddenness*: the hidden years in Nazareth offer a valuable insight into the mystery of believing. Thirdly it is about *vocation and obedience* – Mary's 'Yes' to God. It is these things which provide a framework for those who come on pilgrimage, enabling them to be receptive in a quite distinctive way to the grace of God. Healing at all other levels remains a central part of the work of Walsingham. This can be emotional, physical, social, spiritual. The channel for this work is generally liturgical, ministered through the sacrament of the sick in the laying-on of hands in anointing and, distinctively at the Anglican Shrine, through sprinkling with water from an ancient well. The person whose story follows is just one among the many thousands who seek that grace in England's Nazareth each year. Her name and background have obviously been changed but she represents every pilgrim seeking for renewal and healing.

Anna comes from the North of England. She described her pilgrimage to Walsingham in the early autumn of 1996 as a 'gentle miracle'. Many aspects of Anna's story have been far from gentle. In the context of ordinary life she had experienced serious ill-health which had led to three major operations in the couple of years prior to her pilgrimage. Illness of that kind is very often far more than simply physical disorder; it can affect the whole outlook of our lives. In Anna's case it became the cause of far deeper suffering. In 1993 she was confronted by the sudden death of her husband. They had been a close family, with two very lively children still at home at the time of Graham's death. Illness and bereavement together led to the break-up of the family and estrangement.

At this low point in her life Anna suffered another devastating tragedy: she was mugged and raped. When Anna came to Walsingham she was very unsure of what she was looking for. In a formal conversation she would have found it difficult to articulate all her feelings of loss, anger and violation. This inability to articulate was itself expressed by a withdrawal from human contact and society. Anna had become little more than a face in the crowd; she was a person who took little or no part in the life of the society around her.

In the rite of the laying-on of hands and anointing with the oil of the sick as it is celebrated at Walsingham, pilgrims are invited to tell the priest who ministers to them what it is they are seeking. A name or phrase is all that's needed, but it matters greatly that people articulate the cause of their hurt or that of those they love. For Anna this was an important moment. In the gentle but formal moment of sacramental encounter she was offered an opportunity to express all the turmoil within. In a strange way, the request to state simply a name or phrase liberated her from the need to explain and therefore made it possible for her to articulate. The particularity was known to God, owned by Anna and shared with the minister of God's love in the Church's ministry to the sick. Here the large gathering became a cradle in which faith and confidence were nurtured so that individual encounter could take place. The pilgrim community secured the safety of those who were vulnerable and isolated.

Initiation into the pilgrim community is something else which is celebrated as part of the ministry to the sick at Walsingham. Part of the burden of Anna's plight was the isolation it imposed. Bereavement and the break-up of her family brought inevitable and natural feelings of being estranged. The rape had reinforced this sense and clouded Anna's mind with feelings of guilt, anger, self-hatred, hatred of others, guilt about her hatred etc.

Baptism is the sacrament in which a whole life story is embraced and incorporated into the life of Jesus Christ, in his mystical body, the Church, 'the blessed company of all faithful people' as the *Book of Common Prayer* puts it. For Anna this meant being able to recognize her place among this faithful people, and renewal of her incorporation was an important element in the work of healing in her life. In the Anglican Shrine at Walsingham there is an ancient well. It was discovered quite by chance when the foundations for the present building were being laid in 1931. Pilgrims come to be sprinkled with water from the well, which they receive in three ways: first as a sip to drink, then in the sign of the cross marked on their forehead, and finally a little is poured into their hands. The remembrance of baptism is inescapable and for many this is the renewing experience which brings with it thanksgiving for the forgiveness which is assured us when we turn to Christ. But there are other levels at which this works.

The water poured into pilgrims' hands can be a reminder of tears, those powerful expressions of the very deepest human emotion, often beyond the control of our mind and will. Tears can be the signs of a hidden life which no one else ever sees, whose full anguish can be obscure even to our own understanding. The nature of her experiences meant that Anna's hurts were hidden – certainly from other people, and to some degree from herself, perhaps as a way of coping. Sprinkling at the well was yet another opportunity for Anna to articulate something about her need for healing. The tears supplied for her from the well symbolized the gift of grace which enables us to do that which it would be impossible for us to do alone.

Walsingham is known as 'England's Nazareth' because the Shrine there incorporates a simple building which represents the setting of the annunciation. Anna discovered a renewed sense of vocation on her pilgrimage to Walsingham which enabled her to return to her home town with new dignity and hope. The large gathering had provided a context through which God had been able to minister to her very personally.

Not long after the pilgrimage I received a letter asking for prayers of thanksgiving to be offered for this 'gentle miracle'. The letter went on to say that during her visit Anna had felt supported and valued as never before and had sufficient confidence in that to come forward for the laying-on of hands and anointing, which physical contact would hitherto have made impossible. A month ago, such a thought would have seemed ridiculous!

The life of the Blessed Virgin Mary is an extraordinary example of how God chooses what the world considers of little significance to be the means by which his glory is revealed. Those who form the pilgrimage gatherings at Walsingham are often frail, sick or damaged in some way. Aware of their weakness, they become aware also of their vocation to be the instruments by which the glory and power of God may be revealed today. We use the following prayer to ask that this work might continue in the lives of all who seek healing and renewal at the Shrine:

God our Father, form in us the image of your Son, and deepen his life with us. Send us as witnesses of gospel joy into a world of fragile peace and broken promises. Touch the hearts of all men and women with your love, that we in turn may love you and one another. We ask this in the name of Jesus the Lord. Amen.

2. Spring Harvest   *Graham Gilliland*

Spring Harvest is always held over the Easter period. It sees as its primary purpose the equipping of the Church, a task it seeks to do in a variety of ways – acknowledging the importance of seeing Christians in a holistic way, body, mind and spirit, and accepting the importance of using all the gifts God has given us, not just the more acceptable academic ones. Each day has a full programme of bible teaching, seminars, times of worship, and also times to relax a little – and the teaching is supplemented by study and seminar notes, tapes, videos and books. Thus the impact continues throughout the year, as tapes are listened to and lent to others. Speakers are drawn from a variety of standpoints and denominations, and they are not allowed to preach their own party line. Thus those running the event wish to give the Holy Spirit every opportunity to reach and touch hearts and lives, without any hype or attempts to force people to take part in something with which they are not comfortable. In fact, the differences between people's standing on the subject of renewal is respected and even catered for, with different styles of worship on offer. One of the greatest effects the event has had on the Church must be in the area of worship, for the full impact of thousands singing their hearts out to God in unity is immensely powerful, and often moves those taking part to tears.

My first visit to Spring Harvest was at Minehead in 1995 and I was, quite frankly, extremely sceptical and even nervous. My church background – Northern Irish Presbyterian – made me wary of anything that might be at all emotional. But my girl friend had been going for ten years, and with her assurance that it would be fine, I went!

From the first night I was there, I loved it. I only had to go into the tent and I knew that something special was happening; I knew God was there. The atmosphere, the people worshipping; it was real, not emotional – you only had to look at the people's faces; it was tremendous. The more meetings I went to, the more it reached my heart. There was an excellent balance between spiritual enjoyment and worship as well, and I had never known such peace. I felt God speak to me about spiritual maturity and tell me that Christianity is something we are meant to enjoy, not just something to believe in. In my church life, I had always been told 'You must believe these things' – about God, Christ, the cross and so on, and I always had believed them. I knew they were true, but that was as far as it went. Now at Spring Harvest I learnt that these things are not only true but you can enjoy them.

I had always been taught before that the gifts of the Spirit were for the apostolic time only, and that the Church had only needed the gifts of tongues, prophecy etc., in its infancy. These were signs attesting to the apostles' calling, which had died with the apostles themselves. There seemed also to be a fear of the gifts of the Spirit, and even a condescending approach to those who claimed to have spoken in tongues or received a touch from God to heal them. As far as receiving the Holy

Spirit himself (the 'baptism of the Holy Spirit'), there was an attitude of 'I got it all at conversion'. Any other experience subsequent to conversion must be from another source. There was also a sense that renewal in the Holy Spirit had more to do with emotions than anything else. So whenever I heard of the Holy Spirit moving in some remarkable way, I would have nothing to do with it! But at Spring Harvest I learnt that God really wants to do a radical thing in people's lives, for us to take hold of the realities of the Christian faith and have a life of joy through them. When I am worshipping at Spring Harvest, God reminds me time and again of the verse, 'If the Son shall set you free, you shall be free indeed'. I have realized that God wants me not so much to know about him as to know him. More and more I have come to realize that the Holy Spirit is a living person who wants to pour his renewing power into our lives. I have also come into a greater reverence for God, yet also paradoxically a greater openness and freedom in his presence. My views of God and the Holy Spirit are not as lopsided as they once were. For me, Spring Harvest has got the balance right between Spirit and truth, between experience and doctrine – it doesn't stress one at the expense of the other.

When I returned home, people said, 'You've enjoyed it, haven't you?' They could tell by the look on my face. I've come home with a greater ability to witness, particularly at work (I work for the Inland Revenue, with a lot of non-Christians). There was such joy welling up in my heart that I didn't need to say anything – they could see the radical difference it had made. And I have a greater joy in witnessing; things are real to me, in a way that I never knew before – it's such a liberating experience. I knew I was saved, but Christianity isn't just fire insurance, it isn't just about getting away from hell. I came back wanting to serve God more and more, wanting to live a holy life for him. My best friend was as sceptical about Spring Harvest as I had been, but he came along and now he loves it too.

To their credit, the folk in my church were most gracious in their reactions when I came home. They later said they could see how changed and moved I was by the experience of going to Spring Harvest, and so there must be something in it. My minister, although he would hold to the teaching outlined above, was most encouraging and gracious in his attitude. I think the general feeling was, 'We disagree with the general tone of the event, and are surprised you went, but how can we criticize something that is evidently so real?' The main opposition I encountered came from Christians outside my denomination, who felt that I was betraying the 'reformed cause' by turning 'charismatic'. As I explained what had happened to me, most opposition ceased. I think some despaired, and others perhaps were jealous not to have this new-found freedom. I found the passages in Acts 1.4-8, 8.14-15 and 19.1-2 very helpful when explaining to people that receiving the Holy Spirit is a reality to be lived out and experienced in one's life. And the experience I received is not just a fleeting thing, but is undergirded by such rich and solid bible teaching. This is the thing that I look forward to most at Spring Harvest, because the teaching shows that it is not just a frothy experience-oriented event, but rather experience backed up by in-depth teaching. When I have received so much teaching, it is wonderful to go and express my thankfulness to God in a meaningful way through worship.

God has taught me, through Spring Harvest, that believing in grace is one thing, but living in the joy of it is another. It has been a humbling experience, and I long for others to share it. I even have more peace over the political situation in Northern Ireland. Whereas once I used to pray with a sense of hopelessness, now I know God is in control of everything and can intervene, can soften the hardest of hearts. He did it for me and he can do it for others as well. I am so grateful that God has shown me that my Christian faith is something to be enjoyed, and that expression of new-found joy has given me the opportunity to witness to others (both Christians and non-Christians) of what it means to live in the fullness of the Holy Spirit.

3.   New Wine   *Karen Sherman*

Whilst maintaining orthodox Christian doctrine, New Wine emphasizes certain specific practices to promote the renewal of the Church through the Holy Spirit. Worship is a key feature of these gatherings. Also, much time is devoted to what is generally termed 'ministry'. This may be in the large central gatherings or in the context of the many seminars held during the week. This prayer ministry is exercised by a trained team of more than 500 who pray with people for every aspect of wholeness – body, mind and spirit – including a living faith in Jesus Christ. The style of the worship and ministry is modelled on that originally encouraged by the late John Wimber, whose teaching on the healing ministry has had such a profound effect on charismatic evangelicals.

My story of renewal owes much to New Wine. I was born in the 1940s, the grand-daughter of a missionary in Sri Lanka who later became vicar of Crondall Church in Surrey. None of my family were 'religious' but we dutifully went to church at Christmas and Easter. At boarding school from the age of twelve, I went weekly to the parish church in Sussex in Sunday-best clothes. It was a day to which none of us looked forward. I was duly confirmed at the age of fourteen, along with the rest of my year. I received a King James Bible and some lovely cards, but I have to say that the true impact of confirmation did not reach me during my teenage years. I married at 22. My husband had been a quiet, faithful Christian all his life, but it was something we never discussed, and although I did accompany him to church some Sundays, I used to come away feeling let down and couldn't understand what there was to attract people. I did feel hypocritical at times, but during our years living in the North, it was what we all did on Sundays; the community life revolved around church and parish meetings, fêtes etc. My husband read his devotional book regularly, and even though I ridiculed him, he took no notice and quietly kept on reading.

When we moved to Somerset in 1984 we joined the local church and served on committees, did flowers, were sidespeople etc. I even learned to play the organ and spent many happy hours on a Saturday morning practising hymns and occasionally playing for services. However, I used to come out of church on those occasional Sundays feeling more depressed than when I went in! In 1989 I went up for prayer at a church which we also attended for special services, but really didn't know why. Maureen, the lady who prayed for me, told me afterwards that she prayed for three and a half years because she knew I would come back one day.

In 1993 we had another difficult year, both financially and with family problems, especially with the behaviour of our son. We felt in need of a holiday, but couldn't afford to go away. We had bought a caravan the year before, and my husband arranged that we would go up the road (six miles) to the Bath and West Showground to a Christian Family Conference called New Wine! He was influenced by two couples who were great friends and were going. I was furious; I didn't know how to face my work colleagues when they asked where I was going for my summer holiday! However, we duly arrived and I was even more angry when I discovered how much we had paid to get into this event. There were over 7,000 people there, and after the first hour I was quite convinced that they were all mad, as the leaders, with hundreds of people in tow, walked around the perimeter of the site praying and singing spiritual songs.

The first evening celebration was even more shocking; most people seemed to have their eyes closed and waved their arms in the air – most extraordinary. I felt very conspicuous standing like a soldier to attention, but realized that they were not actually worried about what I was doing or not doing. We went to some seminars, and I began to hear the truth about Jesus for the first time and learn more about Christianity.

On that third afternoon we went to a seminar on the Beatitudes and the Lord's Prayer. My husband dozed off in the hot marquee. However, something dramatic was happening inside me and at the end of the session, as we walked out, my heart caught on fire. I suddenly turned to my husband and said, 'That's it then – it's simple really – I am going to give my life to Jesus!' At that moment the Holy Spirit completely deluged me (and I didn't even know what it was!). I felt completely transformed. It was as if I had fallen in love with Jesus, and it was so huge and so overwhelming that I didn't know what to do with it. I literally rushed to the nearest stall to buy a cross and a Bible, and spent all night and the rest of the week reading and reading, so much so that my husband got fed up with being nudged awake late at night whilst I excitedly read passages from it to him.

That night we went into the celebration and sang the Lord's Prayer, and the tears started to flow and dropped in big pools at my feet as my eyes saw for the first time the beauty, joy and love of Jesus and knew that he had given me new life. Those friends around me who had been praying for me watched as I raised my hands in love and adoration to Jesus.

However, a few weeks later some unpleasant things started to happen: storms broke over me and inside me, pain and depression swamped me in waves. I had no knowledge of repentance and forgiveness or how to live a Christian life in victory over the spiritual enemy. This enemy had a field day with me. He was determined not to give up, and I felt I could not cope any more. There were huge areas of my life which were full of unhealed pain and anger, and I experienced enormous pain as they were given to Jesus and laid at the foot of the cross. We have dear Christian friends with a wonderful healing ministry who lovingly and thoroughly helped me deal with the past. There were many subtleties in the tactics used by the enemy to entice me away from my new faith, from cynical, sceptical books which became compulsive reading, to direct lies and attacks by family and friends. It became unbearable to read or touch my bible; I couldn't go to church or pray, and I felt so alone and far away from God. I wouldn't even wear my cross. My husband was extremely concerned and somewhat frightened at the sudden and unexplicable change of behaviour and did not know how to handle the harsh voice and unpalatable words which were being emitted. In the end in desperation he escaped to sensible friends for advice and prayer.

After several hours he returned to find me in a frenzy of pain, but a strong Christian friend in London telephoned, ostensibly out of the blue. As I poured out the whole sorry story of the demise of my short-lived faith and loss of Jesus, he prayed fervently down the phone and a blessed release came.

I was restored by the Lord that night into an even stronger relationship with him, and although that was a bad time, since that first difficult autumn my faith has grown. I never cease to be amazed and excited at how God leads us through the darkness and heals us, and then sends us in directions which we never could have imagined in our wildest dreams – the Christian life is full and life giving. The Lord has led us to a church in which we thrive, where we receive love and care and in turn minister to others, and I am doing what he has gifted and anointed me to do – playing for him in worship. It is a privilege to be able to serve the Lord.

For reflection

1.   Which of the three large gatherings described above attracts you most?

2.   What particular feature of that gathering appeals to you?

3.   Are there practical steps you can take to explore this aspect further?

4.   Spend some moments reflecting on the way water is used at Walsingham. Are there imaginative ways in which water could be employed in your own devotions and/or in the life of your church?

5.   As you reflect on Graham's experience at Spring Harvest, is it your experience that your faith is true in your mind, but not so much in your heart? You might like to spend some time praying for the Holy Spirit to come and help you with that journey of liberation from mind to heart.

6.   Karen's experience at New Wine had to do with 'falling in love' with Jesus. If you wish, spend some time opening your heart in love to Jesus. You may like to use hymns, songs, prayers, silence, a cross or crucifix, icon etc. – whatever you find helps you most.

Resources

Walsingham

For further information about pilgrimage to Walsingham please write to: The Administrator, The College, Walsingham, Norfolk, NR22 6EF (Tel/Fax: 01328 820266).

Spring Harvest

Write to: Spring Harvest, 14 Horsted Square, Uckfield, East Sussex TN22 1QL (Tel: 01825 769111; Fax: 01825 769141).

New Wine

Information on New Wine family and youth events can be obtained from: New Wine Trust, 37 Quickley Lane, Chorleywood, Herts WD3 5AE (Tel: 01923 446655).

Over the years other conferences have grown out of New Wine, including Lakeside (a long weekend for the family), Soul Survivor (for teens and twenties) and many others directly or indirectly in this country and abroad. In addition New Wine Trust runs leaders' days, retreats and teach-ins, as well as establishing regional relational networks across the UK of church leaders with a common commitment to prepare for revival.

6

Renewal through initiation

Introduction

During the 1990s, one fact that has come home loud and clear to the Church is that the long era of Christendom in the West has come to an end. The days when we could assume that most people in Britain would have at least a passing knowledge of the Ten Commandments and the Lord's Prayer have ended. We are now seeing new generations emerging in this land who know as much about Islam, Hinduism and Judaism as they do about Christianity, and often this knowledge is limited and confused. We can no longer assume that children will leave school with a clear knowledge of what the Christian faith is about.

As a result of this religious and cultural change, the Church is finding that it is having to engage not only in new missionary endeavours, but also, in conjunction with evangelism, in clear apologetics and systematic teaching about the Christian faith. Many who are coming to faith in Christ are doing so without a Christian background and therefore need to be clearly instructed in the Christian faith. Furthermore, those who have been regular members of a church for many years are also ignorant of many fundamentals of the Christian faith. In short, we are discovering that it is not simply conversion that is required, but effective initiation into the Christian faith, teaching the beliefs and values of Christianity, that will lead to an ongoing transformation. In the light of this, there have been a number of new programmes designed to educate people in the faith and equip them with all that they need to live a full Christian life and to be effective witnesses in our post-Christian society. There are a variety of courses now on offer and, as we shall see in this chapter, the experience of many is that engaging with such courses is proving to be a way of renewal.

This chapter includes three stories from three different initiation courses that have developed over the years. *Dorothy Lacy* tells us about her experience a few years ago with the course *Saints Alive!* This six-week course was written in the 1980s by Bishop John Finney and Felicity Lawson when they were both at St Margaret's Church, Aspley, Nottingham. They were both keen to develop a short, easy to use course that would both give clear instruction about the Christian faith and also help people to a proper appreciation and experience of the work of the Holy Spirit in their lives. They passed it on to Anglican Renewal Ministries, who published and promoted it. It has become an excellent preparation course for confirmation, but has been used much more widely than that. Hundreds of thousands of people have completed this course in several different countries, and for many it has been a key to personal and church renewal.

The second story has been provided by *Revd Canon Clarry Hendrickse* who is Vicar of Christ Church, Eccleston, a suburb of St Helens, Merseyside, in the Liverpool Diocese. He writes about the now famous *Alpha* course. This is a ten-week introductory course to the Christian faith. It originated at Holy Trinity Brompton (often known as 'HTB') and combines teaching on basic doctrine with practical pastoral insights into how to read the Bible, pray, etc. As run at HTB, Christians bring their friends and relatives to a fairly lavish introductory supper, at which the course is explained and people invited to attend. Nicky Gumbel, a clergyman on the staff at HTB, presently runs the courses. Prior to ordination he was a barrister in London. His talks are available as audio tapes or videos, and written up in his book *Questions of Life*. His book *Telling Others* explains fully the thinking behind the course. Both are published by Kingsway. Clarry gives us Susan's story and her experience of renewal through doing the course.

Our third story is about the relatively new *Emmaus* course. This course has been produced by a team of writers: Felicity Lawson, John Finney, Robert Warren, Steve Croft and Stephen Cottrell. It is a three-stage nurture course. Stage 1 gives guidance on how to make contact with those who are enquiring about the Christian faith, and how to form a group. Stage 2 is a fifteen session initial engagement with the Christian faith. There is then a third stage, a post-initiation resource in four work-books which achieves a more thorough work of discipling. *Revd Mark Beach*, the Vicar of All Hallows, Gedling, in the Southwell Diocese, has provided us with two short stories of people from his parish who have been involved in this course.

1.   Saints Alive!   *Dorothy Lacy*

'Since I went on the Saints Alive! course . . .' is part of many a sentence spoken by people in our church, St John the Baptist, Chapeltown, Sheffield. The course gave us a firm scriptural base for our faith, it allowed us to ask questions and gave us an opportunity to become closer to the clergy and to each other. It is suitable for young and mature Christians as well as for newcomers to church. We learnt how to pray in different ways, in meditation, in intense prayer, through arrow prayers and even in tongues if ordinary words seemed inadequate. And we learnt to pray together – quite a revelation for some of us.

And it has affected relationships. You always have a special feeling for the people who did the course with you and you seem to be on the same wavelength as other Saints Alivers. Some lovely friendships have grown up between young and older members of the congregation. All this has produced a really powerful network of strong, loving relationships throughout the church. This, in turn, must say something to people out-side the church. But don't imagine that all is plain sailing. Wherever God is at work, so is the Devil and there have been some almighty upsets which have rocked us all to our roots – but with God's help we have weathered them.

Perhaps I could illustrate the effect of Saints Alive! on one person by telling you about my husband, *John*, although many others have had equally dramatic experiences. He had dropped out of the post-Billy Graham nurture group in 1985, I think because he found it too intense and threatening. He had suffered from angina since 1977 and often felt really appalling, which made me frantic with worry, and he had suffered abuse from an uncle when he was a child which had set up lifelong stresses and conflict within him, leading to times of deep depression and black moods. He felt such a wretch that he thought God had no time for him. All I could do was pray about him.

After a while the Saints Alive! course was announced, where you could find out more about God and deepen your spiritual life. Our curate assured me that even older people like me could join, so I signed up. Amazingly, John decided he'd give it a go too. So a group of eight met in our house and it was a marvellous experience. Peter, our vicar, taught us well and we could ask questions. We began to catch some of the excitement of the early Church, expecting to meet with God. During the fourth session, I was horrified to see John's head drooping and his eyes closing. There he was, sitting next to the vicar, actually nodding off when he was supposed to be having his spiritual life deepened! He was famous, really, for nodding off at inappropriate times but this was seriously embarrassing! I found myself saying lamely by way of justification, 'It's his angina tablets, you see'!

As the time approached for the session where we were to be prayed for individually in church, I could see John becoming more and more apprehensive – well, we all were. We gathered together in church with gentle music coming from a tape recorder and we were told to come to the front when the time felt right, so that Peter could pray for us. I had made up my mind that I wanted him to pray with me for John's spiritual dilemma and his health as I couldn't bear to see him so upset. Meanwhile, John had gone up to the altar first. I never saw him come back as my eyes were closed by then, but suddenly I had this overwhelming feeling that whatever had been troubling John had been dealt with. Panic set in then! What could I ask to be prayed about now? I didn't need to worry though, for when my time came there was plenty of sinfulness in me that needed sorting!

I felt so excited for John. However, I decided not to ask directly what had happened to him, but to give him some space to tell me in his own time. And sure enough, on the way home, it all came tumbling out – how he'd gone up to the altar and confessed about all the conflicts going on inside him and how, when Peter put his hand on John's head, it was as though a shaft of heat and light shot through him and a great burden was lifted. He was so excited and surprised.

After that, his life seemed to be transformed. He knew that God had accepted him, just as he was. The lovely side of his nature seemed to be far more on top than the darker side. He wanted everyone to share in this wonderful love God had for him. I'm not saying that the problems never resurfaced, because they did, but he knew that God accepts, God forgives and, by repentance, God restores. His life became so exciting and nearly always when the communion wine touched his lips, the familiar shaft of heat and light used to pass through him, almost overwhelming him as he clung to the communion rail, with everyone worried as to whether he was all right, until eventually he'd return to his pew, burning up with the heat.

At the monthly parish prayer meetings, he began having pictures about issues in our church life. He found he was praying in tongues when he couldn't find the words to tell God how much he loved him. I heard him, one day, telling a surprised visitor that 'You can really feel the Holy Spirit crackling round our church at some services, you know'. One night I complained to him that I wished I could share in these spiritual fireworks. I read my bible regularly and tried to pray diligently but, although I had a growing relationship with God, I didn't seem to experience this supernatural side of him. John smiled and said, 'Well, you see, I'm thick, and it's the only way he can get through to me.'

One of our great joys, after the Saints Alive! course, was that we were able to pray together each morning before we got up. I think those times were the closest I ever got to heaven, as we shared together with God our concerns for people and issues. If John was feeling rough with his angina, we would pray about that too – God always honoured our trust and set him right. We always finished our prayers with the Grace and Psalm 23 and each time a different facet of the psalm would strike us and give us food for thought.

The following autumn John's health deteriorated and although he still did the things he loved to do, he was spending longer resting in between. During the few days just before Christmas, he spent a lot of time praying for me, which I found worrying. The day after Boxing Day, I had to send for the doctor as John was having chest pains. After the doctor had gone, I went upstairs, to find John really excited. 'That doctor was a Christian, you know. Did you hear what he said? "God bless you"!'

That night John died from a massive heart attack and was safe with the God who loves him. During his funeral service, we were all given an opportunity for silent prayer. Suddenly I had this vivid picture of a tiny, brilliantly-lit John sitting on God's huge, silvery knee, waving joyfully and saying 'I'm alright' – and, of course, he is.

2.   The Alpha course   *Clarry Hendrickse*

I am Vicar of Christ Church, Eccleston. The congregation is mostly professional/managerial, but we also have some from the council housing. We have benefited greatly from the Alpha course. The course provides videos of Nicky Gumbel's presentation of the Christian faith. For us it was an advantage to have a very gifted outside speaker who, despite his obvious Oxbridge background, seems able to communicate across different cultures to a whole range of people. After the video we had a tea break and then discussion groups. Present at our courses were church members and their friends, which included some from a nearby council estate. We also had a group just for couples getting married and a group who were doing it as confirmation training. All expressed appreciation at the way they had greatly benefited from Alpha. It has also been enlightening to see the number of established church members who for the first time have come to an understanding of the basic tenets of their Christian faith.

On the video, the relaxed atmosphere at HTB and the manner of Nicky Gumbel's presentation communicates Christian truths in a way that retains people's interest without judging or threatening them, and the length of the course allows the time which most people need to consider seriously the claims of Christ. On the minus side, the videos made soon after the Toronto Blessing had come across the Atlantic seem insensitive to those who find 'the ministry of the Holy Spirit' difficult in any way and these had an unnecessarily negative effect on a number of people on the course. This has apparently been remedied in later, revised, tapes.

The way the subject of Christian healing is presented again relies heavily on the John Wimber model and has all the impressiveness and limitations of putting all one's eggs into that particular basket. The location of HTB means that they have access to large numbers of the population and can sustain a rolling programme of three courses every year. It is my experience, and the experience of three clergy colleagues in St Helens, that the number of people who come on the second and subsequent courses is greatly reduced and most of us now run a maximum of two a year, with one church having just a few new people doing the course in a house group. But as my colleague put it, 'Even having three or four new Christians join our church each time makes it worth doing.' Alpha has had the effect of bringing a new confidence in the gospel to many established church members, as well as a new sense of the reality of the presence of God; and a good number of people distant from God have come to a new understanding of Christ's claims upon their lives. The story of *Susan* which follows is not untypical of the amazing things we have seen the Holy Spirit do in and through those who put themselves in the way of this form of renewal.

Susan is 37, married to Jack, and has two children aged 10 and 7. She has been attending church for the past eight years since they moved into the parish. She decided that her daughter ought to attend Sunday School and so felt obliged to set an example. She thought of herself, but not her husband, as Christian, the difference in her mind being that she had been confirmed but he had not, although he had been baptized. She does childminding, helps with a playgroup and promotes the advantages of breast feeding. Jack works as a projects manager for a major national firm and often brings paperwork home in the evenings and at weekends.

When her grandmother died three years ago Susan was with her in the hospital and felt that something had gone out of her. It made her think for the first time about where her Grandma had actually gone. She jumped at the chance to join an Alpha course. It offered her the opportunity to ask all her unanswered questions. To begin with, she just found it interesting, especially when she began to understand the background to the Bible; but then, in her words, she 'got caught up in it all'. She enjoyed the group discussions and mixing with Christians who already had a relationship with God. She bought a modern Bible which she found she could read easily and understand. When she had tried to read an Authorized Version and been unable to understand it, she had assumed that the problem was her. When she had previously read the Bible she had thought that

> it had all happened then and I hadn't realized that it still worked today. People talking about what God was doing in their lives yesterday and today made it all real, believable, accessible to me. It suddenly dawned on me that he was accessible to everybody. It's not just the likes of Isaiah that God speaks to. He speaks to us all.

There was no particular turning-point in Susan's experience. In fact, not so much a turning-point as a confirmation that God was there for her. When I asked her to say something about her experience of Alpha at a church service, her immediate response was 'There's no way I could do anything like that'. But she began to feel uneasy about her decision and, reading a book by Adrian Plass about Gideon, she asked God for a sign. She had given several reasons why she was unable to respond, a key one being that her elderly and sickly parents were expected for dinner on the day she had been asked to say something. Within minutes of her request to God, her father rang to say that they would unexpectedly be unable to come. It seemed to her to be the obvious and simple sign she needed. As soon as her father said it, she felt she had to accept the invitation to speak in church, and with that resolution she felt that a weight had been lifted off her. In the event, although she had made copious notes which she intended to read, she spoke extremely well without reference to them. She says that it felt as though God was holding her in a bubble of his love.

Since completing the Alpha course at Easter Susan says that her whole attitude to life has changed. This Christmas, for example. The family normally spent Christmas Day by themselves, perhaps inviting her parents. She has two married brothers with grown-up families whom they have hitherto tried to avoid seeing apart from birthdays. This year the family had become much more important and she felt compelled to invite all of them for Christmas. Not all of them were able to accept, but Susan feels that she has started on a new way of relating which will help them all to grow closer together in the years to come. She now reads the Bible and prays every lunch time as well as speaking to God at odd moments during the day as she works around the house. 'If I have to miss it, I feel a hunger – like having missed a meal.' She finds her children talking more about God because she does.

Jack supports Susan inasmuch as he supports her in everything. She said, 'He doesn't object to it, is not against it, but definitely doesn't believe it.' Midway through Alpha she became very anxious that she and Jack 'might end up going to different places'. This fear was eventually resolved by someone pointing out 1 Corinthians 7.14 to her: 'For the unbelieving husband is made acceptable to God by being united to his wife.' She is now aware that she is not just responsible to herself but also answerable to God.

Alpha has also given Susan a whole new awareness and sensitivity. Before, she worried about the homeless for a short time but would then forget them. Now she worries about the homeless and believes she should try to do something about it. She really enjoys going to church and misses it when she cannot go. Jack does not seem to mind because he does his paperwork while she is at church. She used to grope for some coins on her way out of the house to use as collection. Now she gives thoughtfully and proportionately from her own income. She says that it would have been too easy to simply give some of Jack's salary. She has been asked to go on a rota of people who read lessons in church but so far has been unable to accept. She was put off reading aloud at school. She says:

> It's actually reading God's word out loud in church.
> It's a grave responsibility but a great honour. I think
> I will have to start doing it some time but I can't say
> I'm looking forward to it. But if he could help me
> when I spoke before in church, then he can help me
> with this.

3.   Emmaus   *Mark Beach*

For some years now I have watched people take the first steps along a journey of faith but fail to find a way of living it out after the first few months. So I began a search for material that would recognize that faith grows gradually and is nurtured by meeting with a group of people who grow to trust each other, and would provide markers along the journey. The two stories that you are about to read are by two people in very different situations who have participated in Emmaus, and through the course have come to a renewed faith in God.

Jackie Dawn writes: The name 'Emmaus' is highly significant and relates, of course, to the incident in the Bible where two travellers on the road to Emmaus were so caught up in their own despair and disbelief over the death of Jesus that they failed for a long time to recognize that the stranger who walked by their side, sharing their journey, was in fact Jesus himself. They saw Jesus but somehow did not recognize him and, in a way, that pretty well sums up my own experience before the course.

Although I have been involved with All Hallows Church in Gedling for over twelve years, I can honestly say that it is only very recently that I have begun to realize what coming to church is really all about. Emmaus has played a very large part in that for me. When you start coming to church it's easy to be fooled into believing that everyone else sitting in their pews on a Sunday has got all this faith stuff sorted out. Very few people have the courage to question or express doubts in case they look foolish.

It's only when you make time to question and face up to the doubts that you can really start to make sense of this elusive thing called *faith*, and the Emmaus course provides a secure place for everybody to do this. There were two groups meeting, with very different people, all at different stages – some new to church, some returning, some had been coming awhile. Two 'companions' were assigned to each group. I was one of them in our group. Our role as 'companion' was not at all what I expected. I anticipated that we would be the ones to get the discussion going. In reality it has been nothing like this. Very often we could not get a word in edgeways! As a result, I have gained as much from the experience as the group members have, and I feel privileged to have been allowed on the journey along with them.

Within the parish we now have plans to increase the number of people that we can reach through Emmaus and, based on my own experience of coming to a closer faith in God, I know that this is an exciting and extremely rewarding opportunity for all of us to grow in faith.

Eleanor Crossley writes: Looking back on my childhood, I am aware that I had a privileged upbringing, life was good, my family was happy and everything came easily to me. Then, when I was 16 years old, my mother died and my life changed. I became self-sufficient, learnt to deal with things on my own and I didn't need anyone. I was self-assured, strong and confident. How wrong I was. By the time I was 29, I had lost my way, but my life's ambition was to have a family. By the time I was 37 I had four children, a comfortable home and few worries. But I was troubled. Surely there was more to life than this. Perhaps I needed a career, more money, more time to myself, a better relationship. Life held no meaning, no hope, everything was dreary and dark.

The time came for my fourth child to be baptized, and as I hadn't been back to my local church after the baptisms of my other children, I couldn't face the hypocrisy of returning. So I went to All Hallows Church and because it was not my local church, I was asked to attend a few services beforehand to apply for 'out of catchment' transfer. It would be difficult to understate the transformation at that point in my life. A new world opened up, an entirely different way of approaching day-to-day living. I was hungry to know more. I was invited to a newly formed Emmaus Group and with trepidation I went along.

This was a new thing for me. A group of people, some vaguely known, others strangers, meeting to discuss what we thought life was all about. 'Did God exist, Yes or No?' To accept 'No' meant that life is only what you make of it for yourself, and I had not done very well so far. There must be more to life than existing. There must be some reason for me to be the way I am. So the answer must be 'Yes, God does exist'. In our small groups we discussed our feelings, doubts and questions. I found strength to talk about how I felt. It helped to realize that others felt the same, or had felt the same earlier on in their journey of faith. The Emmaus Group began by discussing basic but important questions: 'Is God out there?'; 'Belief in God'; and 'Why the need to worship?'.

At first I found it very difficult even to say 'God'. I had a very high wall which needed to be overcome. I had lived a life of denying that God existed. My family were not churchgoers and I still had to come to terms with why my family life was disrupted when I was younger. The Emmaus Group brought to the surface a lot of long-forgotten feelings of grief and loss. It was like a counselling session. When we reached the Parable of the Lost Son, quite a few members of the group felt great emotion at the spiritual understanding of the parable. A longing to be forgiven for all that was past, to be accepted and held in the arms of a loving and forgiving father. I felt that I had turned round and was heading for home.

We reached the chapter where we were asked about our inner space. I learnt the wonderful expression about the 'God-shaped hole' inside each one of us waiting to be filled. Slowly it was sinking in: the sense of purpose and inner peace was all to do with accepting and loving God. Things were beginning to make sense to me. We spoke about the walls put up by our sinful nature, about pride, guilt and unwillingness to change. I recognized these things in me. My acceptance of God was fine when I was in church or in the presence of like-minded people. But was all this for real when I was on my own? Again I felt a bit of a fake – the walls still needed to be broken down. I had God in my head but was not so sure that I had allowed him into my heart. Our study turned to Jesus and the history of the Bible. In a sense, this to me was the easiest part, to accept a figure in history who existed and fulfilled the prophecies. He died by crucifixion and rose from the dead in three days. But the hard part was to understand that he took the sins of the world on his shoulders so that we might be free. That didn't seem fair somehow.

My study with the Emmaus Group led me to explore my inner self, to find my place in the world alongside other people. I came to realize that I wasn't the only person thinking and worrying about religion and belief. Together we helped each other to take a few steps forward along the journey of faith. Without the opportunity to study together I would not have been able to listen to sermons in this new way, nor would I have grown spiritually or had the courage to go to a prayer conference or even read the Bible. Recently I have felt the need to be absolved of all the sins I have committed in the past, which I now realize have hurt God in his trust in me. What can I do to repay him for his patience in waiting for me to open my heart and allow him to enter my life? The light has been turned on, my future has taken on new meaning and by continuing to study, I hope that I will be able to do God's work in a way that will help others. The Emmaus Group was the turning point, a stepping stone which has helped me to accept God into my life and shown me how to grow both spiritually and physically into a better person.

For reflection

1.   Which of the three initiation courses described above attracts you most?

2.   What particular feature of that course appeals to you?

3.   Are there practical steps you can take to explore it further?

4   A number of people in this chapter have talked about their faith coming alive and becoming relevant to their daily lives. Is there any way in which your faith has become stale? You may like to pray for God the Holy Spirit to come and fan the flame of faith within you.

5.   Does having a partner or other member of the family who is apparently not interested in Christ prevent you from exploring your faith more? Would they be interested in one of the courses mentioned in this chapter?

6.   Emmaus sees the Christian life very much in terms of a journey of discovery. Reflect for a few moments about where you are on your journey. What have been your recent discoveries? What are the questions that are uppermost in your mind?

Resources

Saints Alive!

Write to: Anglican Renewal Ministries, 42 Friar Gate, Derby DE1 1DA (Tel: 01332 200175; Fax: 01332 200185; e-mail: armderby@aol.com).

Alpha

Write to: Holy Trinity Brompton, Brompton Road, London SW7 1JA (Tel: 0171 581 8255; Fax: 0171 589 3390; e-mail: htb.london@dial.pipex.com).

Emmaus

Write to: Bible Society, Stonehill Green, Westlea, Swindon SN5 7DG (Tel: 01793 418100; Fax: 01793 418118; e-mail: info@bfbs.org.uk).

7

Renewal through evangelistic missions

Introduction

Although the focus of an evangelistic mission is the person who has yet to come to faith, the consequence of a church engaging in mission is very often personal and corporate renewal. For those who have not engaged in such a thing, the mention of 'evangelistic missions' conjures up all kinds of images of large football stadia filled with singing choirs and earnest evangelists beckoning people to the front. The past 50 years or so have certainly seen some impressive evangelistic campaigns of this sort, most notably Dr Billy Graham's crusades. On a smaller scale there have been countless university, town and city missions that have gathered large numbers and brought people into a saving knowledge of Christ. There have also been thousands of less prominent local evangelistic campaigns, sometimes based on a local church, sometimes ecumenical, sometimes centred in a school, pub or factory and so on. Increasingly such events have been multimedia, particularly those in the youth culture. Although these events often use a high-profile evangelist, there is often a team involved in both the big events and the ancillary small meetings that often accompany the event.

In our discussions about renewal we recognized that such evangelistic events have had a considerable renewing effect on the Church. In this chapter we have chosen three different expressions of evangelistic missions. Our first contribution is supplied by *Revd Anne Hibbert*, recently appointed as national Millennium Executive, who for some years previously had been on the staff of CPAS. She writes of her involvement in a town mission. She supplies a number of brief stories by people who were involved in the mission. It is particularly encouraging to read these, because some of them were written a year after the mission, indicating the long-term effect of renewal in the lives of these people.

Martin Cavender is one of the *Springboard* team (an initiative by the Archbishops of York and Canterbury on evangelism). He has been closely involved in many different expressions of evangelistic mission through his work with Springboard during the Decade of Evangelism. He tells us about the renewal of faith he experienced in a mission in which he became involved when he was the Diocesan Registrar of Bath and Wells. He also writes about an evangelistic pilgrimage which, though unique, nevertheless gives an insight into the value of an evangelistic mission 'on the move'.

Our third contribution comes from *Revd Stephen Cottrell*, who is the Wakefield Diocesan Missioner and Bishop's Chaplain for Evangelism and also a missioner with Springboard. Stephen writes about the *Mission Weekends* he has been encouraging in his diocese, and how they are within the grasp of even the smallest church. Anyone can do it. It does not cost much, nor does it require years of preparation. It is a very user-friendly concept and, as we shall hear, has proved most effective.

1.   The evangelistic campaign   *Anne Hibbert*

Roger Murphy and I were delighted to be involved with the church at Mancetter, Nuneaton, over a period of eighteen months. The highlight was the special 'Spotlight' week which happened during 1–8 October 1995. Over the months we had had some trial runs with some warm-up events. The organizing committee had worked particularly hard and the people had faithfully prayed. Spotlight itself was a series of home meetings, both in the mornings and afternoons, quiz nights in pubs, a 'Colour, beauty and you' evening and a 'How God changed my life' event by Rosemary Conley. There were also services and a harvest supper plus meals together in people's homes.

Throughout Spotlight we continually met people who were open to the gospel of Jesus Christ. Time and time again people prayed prayers of commitment. Lives were changed. On the Sunday I held an emergency training session because we hadn't got enough nurture group leaders!

Seven follow-up groups were started with about ten people in each. Roger has been back since to talk to them about regular men's outreach events. We are continuing to work with this church while it thinks through its leadership structures and evangelism while an ongoing process in the church's life.

We feel really privileged to have been part of people's experience of spiritual awakening. It feels as though God has taken a huge lid off and just poured in his Spirit. The two key ingredients are partnership and prayer. During the year we have had a follow-up Bible study course and a Lent course, each attended by over 60 people. A year on from the mission we interviewed a number of people who had been involved in it one way or another. The following are a selection of stories.

> I was asked 'What did the Spotlight mission do for me?' Well firstly, I must say it was a pleasure and a privilege to be involved. What did it do for me? Well, after meeting so many wonderful people and listening to them speak, it made me re-evaluate all that I had been taught and believed in for as long as I can remember, but didn't seriously consider – my love for God and the Church. As the week went by, my faith grew stronger, my life took on a new meaning and I am happier and, I hope, a better person for it.

> Can it really be a year since the mission in Mancetter? It doesn't seem that long since Dawn and I made the decision to jump off the fence and make a firm commitment to God. It has been a wonderful year, what with our conference at Swanwick, becoming a member of the PCC and, ultimately, my own confirmation. I never thought I would come so far in such a short space of time and through it all I feel as though I have been gently guided and safe in the knowledge that what I have done has been God's will. The best thing of all is the fact that Dawn made

a commitment as well and we have been able to grow in our love and faith in the Lord together.

What I felt most was the warm and friendly atmosphere at the events I attended. At the time of the mission, I was under a lot of stress following the death of my Dad. When Anne told us of her unhappiness and how she had coped with the help of prayer and her faith, it helped me to realize that I wasn't the only one with problems and there is a way through the black times.

Our lives have changed immeasurably since the Spotlight mission. We have rejoined the church we have always loved and we have enjoyed the friendship of the congregation. However, most importantly, we now live in the love of God. We look forward to the coming years with his love around us.

One of the many things which I have enjoyed since Spotlight '95 is being more involved in the events, group meetings and activities which we have in church, and the fellowship which comes from them.

I had fled to the church during a bad time in my life. I needed help and this was given unstintingly and unreservedly. During Spotlight week, I saw how faith and devotion to God had restored another whose life had been broken. I found myself in the company of people who were like a family and where warmth touched me. There is no light yet out of my darkness, but glimmers of hope now and then appear. I have a lot to learn and a great deal to be thankful for.

Although I had considered myself a Christian, Spotlight renewed my faith in Jesus Christ. The prayer and healing that I received during that week made me very much aware of his presence. The buzz of the Holy Spirit and the warm glow from top to toe was a marvellous experience and one that stays with me. The follow-up of bible classes has been good, reminding us of our need to get together and talk of what we believe. Yes, I think the week of Spotlight and the good team that we had amongst us in prayer, talk and hope for the future in eternal life was good, both for myself and I'm sure many others.

Before the mission, Christianity was just something that we switched on or off when it suited us. The mission taught us that we were able to make the commitment and become Christians without knowing all the answers. We have found that through bible study, worship and prayer, God has become part of our daily lives.

Although we have both attended church on and off all our lives (Freda was a Sunday School teacher for over twelve years), we both feel that since the mission week our faith has expanded at a tremendous rate and we are now more at ease in speaking to family, friends and even acquaintances about all aspects of our Christian beliefs. Prayers have become easier and more spontaneous at any time or anywhere, there is so much more belief in us and we seem to receive much more comfort. The bible studies, both at our home and at the Bracebridge Centre helped us a lot and we can now read the Bible with greater understanding. Wednesday morning prayers have made us more confident in speaking of God's love for us and the power of prayer. We also now feel privileged and happy to belong to the family of St Peter's.

These are just a few brief stories from the mission at Mancetter. There is no doubt that not only were people outside the Church touched by the gospel, but many inside, or on the edges of church life, found a wonderful renewal of their faith by their involvement in this mission.

2.   A mission through pilgrimage   *Martin Cavender*

'Mission' is one of those carry-all words which the Church uses, sometimes to avoid being too precise. 'A mission' is a concept which many in the Church think out-dated, irrelevant to today's culture. Like 'missionary', it conjures up foreign people in dark places; and surely doesn't apply here and now. I believe it does. A simple parish mission made a major difference in my life and, properly related to the local context and culture, I am quite clear that missions (or whatever descriptive word we choose to use) are as vital a part of the life of the Church today as they have ever been. Often, the benefits are as much for the missioners as to those being missioned – certainly that has been true in my case – and the effect can be a renewal and transformation not only for the individual but also for the Church itself. I am sure we need to rediscover the concept of the mission, and use it 'to proclaim the gospel afresh to this generation'.

When I was Registrar in the Diocese of Bath and Wells I was a regular attender at the Diocesan Synods. One warm June meeting in 1984 a note came my way. It read: 'Isn't it about time the Registrar came on a Mission? – Jack.' I was used to receiving notes and questions on little scraps of paper – usually about arcane bits of ecclesiastical law, or some advice to be given or received. This one was quite different; and I must have looked rather flustered to the curious onlookers, as I crumpled it quickly and stuck it in my pocket.

The author of the note was Prebendary Jack Mardon, Diocesan Missioner and Vicar of Locking, near Weston-super-Mare. I didn't know him well, but I knew his formidable reputation. I had seen him offering a presentation to a previous Synod, where he had introduced a butcher who had spoken about having been brought to faith during a recent mission. Jack loved God and talked straight. He was one of that small

111

number of people who produced a stirring in the Synod whenever he rose to speak – whether of apprehension or delighted anticipation it was often difficult to say.

At coffee time I sought him out, took him to a quiet corner and said, 'Jack, I know enough to know that I'm not very far down the road; I'm not a committed Christian.' He replied, 'That's all right! You will be by the time you've been on a Mission.' I could see there was no way out of this one. As I look back on that brief conversation I know that it was one of the defining moments in my life.

My wife Cesca and I had been making our respective ways, mostly together and mostly unconsciously, along the road of faith for some years. We had both come from Christian homes, though Cesca's was more obviously so than mine. The Christian faith had not been in the forefront of our thinking; we had been too wrapped up in family, home-making, business-building and the rest to pay much attention to religion. That was neatly organized into Sundays, plus the bits which came at me through my work for the diocese. With hindsight, my job as Registrar worked more often as a barrier to deeper faith than as a door-way. I was part of the ecclesiastical Establishment, which meant I had a duty to stand up for the Church of England without the risk of anyone asking me too many searching questions about what I *really* believed. What an exquisite irony that this searching question from Jack was coming at me through the ranks of the Synod, that most structural of the bits of the Establishment !

So I agreed to go on a mission, but just 'as an observer', mostly evenings only. The one Jack had in mind was due to happen in the town of Axbridge in the following November, and there would be some training and preparation evenings before then.

My involvement in this mission forced me to clarify my own faith, and I was constantly impressed by the commitment, vitality of faith, humility and humour of the team I was with. They lived a Christian life in a way I did not. So much happened in that mission. We saw many people come to a profession of faith. The queues of people for prayer and ministry ran the length of the parish church at the end of the final service, and many of these people have become members of other mission teams.

There was no blinding flash for me during this mission, but the whole event was a defining moment in my life. I saw God at work and decided that I wanted him to work in my life too. About a month after the mission, around our supper table with some friends, I made the decision for God that has changed my life and the lives of the people around me.

It is not surprising that, following this experience, the theme of mission has been very close to my heart, and I am now working with the Springboard team. This experience has given me many new insights into mission, and there is one that particularly moved me.

In Easter week 1993 a small team set off in a mini-bus to visit all the English cathedrals (except Peel, on the Isle of Man!) during a 16-day period. Preparation had been brief – the idea had only been floated the previous October, and the intervening period had been a scramble of correspondence with deans and chapters and bishops; and then of publicity, printing and the rest. But 42 cathedrals had said 'Yes'. So we set off.

Organized by the relatively new Springboard, the team was led by Bishop Michael Marshall, and comprised a parish priest, around ten theological college students from catholic and evangelical colleges, and two or three others. The plan was to spend an hour in each of three cathedrals per day at 6am, 12 noon and 6pm, in a short offering of proclamation, prayer and praise. On the last day, in London, we managed four cathedrals. We lugged around the 'mighty Wurlitzer' (a keyboard) to accompany the worship, carried an ikon of the Trinity by Anton Rublev, and cast ourselves on the mercy of local organization for most of our beds and meals.

Just over halfway round we came to Liverpool and the amazing Cathedral Church of Christ, set above the city and the docks. We arrived early and so had time to wander around and catch our breaths. Bishop Michael was strolling in a side aisle of the Cathedral when he came across a young man called Richard. They fell into conversation and Michael explained what the team was about. He invited Richard to come to the service and left it there.

Richard came to the service and then stayed on for supper with the team afterwards – thanks to the generosity of the Dean and Chapter.

Conversation flowed, and it was suggested that he might like to join the pilgrimage. We were off to spend the night in Chester. We said to him, 'If you would like to join us, come along with your suitcase to Chester Cathedral at 6am tomorrow!'

Richard came, and stayed with us for the rest of the journey! It had a profound effect on him. Brought up in a loving Christian home, he had wandered away from the faith and was only in Liverpool Cathedral that day because he had heard it was worth seeing the stunning architecture. He found himself caught up in a mission which included people who believed fervently in their faith, came from strikingly different traditions, and were walking together in a work of evangelism which was clearly touching hearts and minds. He saw the Holy Spirit in operation on the road, among the team, and with those who were wanting to join us at each of the cathedrals. By Chichester he had seen all he needed to see and came to a gloriously renewed faith in St Richard's Chapel during our simple team eucharist, following the morning worship. He continues to follow the Lord.

3.   Mission Weekends   *Stephen Cottrell*

'Give, and there will be gifts for you: a full measure, pressed down, shaken together, and overflowing' (Luke 6.38). A rather stale old argument lumbers on about the purpose of parish missions. Are they about inreach or outreach? The answer, of course, is both. A mission that aims to build up the faithful will bear fruit in renewed witness. A mission that aims to share the faith with others will renew the faith of those doing the sharing. The question for missions is not what they aim to achieve – inreach *and* outreach – but how they achieve their aims. Missions cost a lot. They are years in the preparing. Outsiders are invited in to do what is properly the work of insiders. It has been famously said that the Church does not have missions, the Church *is* a mission.

Well, there is another way of looking at this. In the missionary diocese of Wakefield, after years of trying to get local churches to think seriously about the processes of evangelism, we came to the (hardly earthshattering) conclusion that it is a pretty boring process that does not have one or two exhilarating events along the way. Also, a good event is a very efficient way of kick-starting a process. But the event has to be such that it fits into an ongoing strategy and is not so all-consuming that there is no time or energy left for anything else. I suppose we also wanted churches to *do* some evangelism. Even just a little bit. It is so easy to talk about it and theorize about it, so easy to find a hundred good reasons why it should be put off until 'we are ready', but in the end the only way to discover the real issues about evangelism is actually to have a go. And this, of course, will be enormously renewing for the faith of those who try. It is in giving we receive.

Parishes were invited to consider having a 'Mission Weekend'. This would only need a few months' planning, would not cost much money, would only need a small amount of outside help (this to facilitate the gifts already present in the congregation) and would, therefore, build the evangelistic *events* of a mission into the ongoing *process* of becoming a missionary church. The mission would no longer be a bolt-on activity, but a critical part of a missionary strategy.

Here is the story of what happened in one parish: St Michael's, Emley. Emley is a village community between Wakefield and Huddersfield with a fairly small, but growing, worshipping community. Their Mission Weekend is typical of what is now happening with a growing number of churches in our diocese. They are being renewed in mission by putting on a mission.

A small mission team – about six people – was set up in the parish. I met with them and we discussed aims for the weekend. It was recognized that, for most people, becoming a Christian is best understood as a journey; and like all journeys it would probably take time and contain different stages. It was also clear that most people in Emley had hardly started the journey at all. They may have had some belief in God, but they did not see this as having any relevance to daily life. It therefore seemed unlikely that they were going to move from a position of good-natured unbelief to committed faith all at once, over the course of one weekend – though this does happen to a few people. The primary aim of the mission was therefore simply to *make contact with as many of these people as possible.*

Some people had already started the journey, but were still a long way from commitment. The second aim of the mission was to *strengthen contact with those on the fringes of the church and challenge them to go a bit further*. Those of us who attend church regularly are also still on the journey. There is no point in this life when any of us can say we have arrived. We all need to carry on moving in our faith.

The final aim of the mission was to *renew the faith of the church by encouraging people to share their faith with others.* This third aim committed the church to serious spiritual preparation: What is the faith we have to share? With whom could we share it?

The rest of the planning was concerned with organizing events for the Mission Weekend that would best achieve these aims, and an ongoing process that would build effectively on whatever happened. Therefore, an important question was this: When we make contact with someone, or help someone on the fringe to go a bit deeper, how can we provide the next best step for that person to take? It is in answering this vital follow-up question that the event and the process of mission knit together. The problem for big missions is that they inevitably become so concerned with putting on the event that the more strategic long-term questions get put off. A Mission Weekend, because of its smaller scale, begins with these questions and plans the events of the mission around them. The first planning question is: What do we do when the weekend finishes?

The events that were planned in Emley were small, focused and repeatable. To make contact with those outside the church each home group agreed to put on one small event on the Saturday of the weekend. These varied from a coffee morning to raise money for Christian Aid to an afternoon ramble and barbecue for young families.

To encourage those on the fringe, a social evening was held in the upper room of the pub opposite the church. (There is good biblical precedent for the Church meeting in upper rooms.) Members of the congregation were asked to bring a friend or neighbour, and fringe members of the church received a specific invitation. The evening consisted of a quiz, live music from a jazz band, a short testimony from a member of the church, and a talk from an outside speaker, one of the Wakefield Diocesan Lay Evangelists. Everyone present filled in a response form to say what they had made of the evening. As this was the first of its kind put on by the church, it was good to have people's feedback. There was also an opportunity on the form for people to say whether they would like to find out more about the Christian faith. This open way of wording the question meant that Christians, non-Christians and not-sures could all answer the question. Quite a number did, and the week following the Mission Weekend a small enquirers' group started meeting.

To build up the faithful, a special Mission Service was held on the Sunday evening. Everyone in the church was encouraged to think deeply about their own faith. The first part of the service was a presentation of the gospel using role play and drama as well as music, testimony and preaching. When this finished the service did not so much end as change direction. A large cross was placed at the front of the church and everyone was encouraged to come out of their seat and place a candle around the cross as a sign of their desire to bear the light of Christ crucified. Then it was possible for people to receive prayer or ministry or make their confession as they wanted. The service ended when the last person left the church some 90 minutes later.

The weekend at Emley was called 'Looking Up, Reaching Out'; it was a weekend of mission set within a process of renewal and evangelism. Only one event of the weekend – the pub evening – was specifically evangelistic, but all of it was raising the vision of the church – looking up to God – and focusing ministry on the needs of the people of the parish – reaching out. The events on Saturday were about making contact and showing the church to be a concerned, welcoming and witnessing community. The worship events on Sunday were about refreshing the faithful. That Sunday evening many people made a fresh commitment to Jesus.

This rolled into a follow-up programme of enquirer groups, and over the next couple of years the individual events of the weekend became part of the ongoing life of the church. The renewal found in this type of mission is fourfold.

First, *it was renewing just to do the mission.* Not to talk about it but get on and do it. This in itself raised the morale of the church.

Secondly, *many individuals did make a fresh commitment.* In too many churches the weekly round of worship cannot provide the challenge of a moment to make a response or a fresh commitment. This is needed in the life of every church; a time of mission provides the opportunity.

Thirdly, for those engaged in the specific events of the mission, either putting them on or inviting friends, *this was a was a watershed in their life of faith.* What had been theory for so long became lived experience. I led the weekend, but was not present all the time, nor for all the events. Only the pub evening and the Sunday evening worship used outsiders, and even then local church members were heavily involved. It was a mission for the local parish by the local church, facilitated by the diocese using one or two specialists to help encourage, motivate and train. This involvement of ordinary people in evangelism is costly. In order to bring renewal in mission some people are sometimes frightened away. I was not aware of this happening in Emley, but I have known it happen else-where.

Fourthly, *the whole mission strategy of the church was renewed.* Thinking big had made them feel small. They had ended up doing not very much at all. But doing small – a Mission Weekend – had set them on the road to becoming big: a full measure, pressed down, shaken together, and overflowing.

For reflection

1. Which of the three types of mission described above attracts you most?

2. What particular feature of that mission appeals to you?

3. Are there practical steps you can take to explore it further?

4. If you have held a mission in your parish, reflect on how valuable it was. What worked well, and what was not effective?

5. If you have not held a mission in your parish, what style of mission do think would suit you? What would your parish need to get going in mission?

6.   How do you personally feel about being engaged in mission? You might like to spend some time in prayer asking God to fill you with his love and boldness for mission.

Resources

The evangelistic campaign

CPAS are willing to assist with campaigns of the sort described by Anne Hibbert. Their address is: CPAS, Athena Drive, Tachbrook Park, Warwick CV34 6NG (Tel: 01926 334242; Fax: 01926 337613; e-mail: mail@cpas.org.uk).

A mission through pilgrimage

For information about Springboard write to: Springboard, 4 Old Station Yard, Abingdon, Oxon OX14 3LD (Tel: 01235 553722; Fax: 01235 553922).

Mission Weekends

For information about the Wakefield Mission Weekends, write to the Diocesan Office at: Church House, 1 South Parade, Wakefield WF1 1LP (Tel: 01924 371802).

8

Renewal through social action

Introduction

As we gathered our stories of renewal together we found that there were many people who had experienced personal renewal through becoming engaged in some kind of social action. Whilst some were discovering renewal through a Christian conference or prayer meeting, others were discovering it serving broken humanity. Through their encounters with the suffering and the wounded, they discovered a profound spiritual renewal taking place within them. Perhaps it is these who are truly experiencing the renewal described in Ezekiel 47. This is Ezekiel's vision of the water flowing from the temple out into the desert and beyond to the stagnant waters. It is an archetypal picture of renewal, and yet contradicts many understandings of renewal. For although this renewal begins in the temple, the water is actually at its most shallow when it is in the sanctuary. It is when the water is in the desert that it is at its deepest. Ezekiel's renewal is not about dwelling in religious meetings. It is about going out to the barren places and discovering there the depths of the Spirit. In terms of this analogy, the place to discover the deep waters of renewal is not in church, but in the places of broken humanity beyond the sanctuary of Christian worship. Though it begins in the place of worship, it leads elsewhere. The following three stories describe most movingly such experiences of renewal discovered in some of the places of suffering in our society.

In this chapter we explore three very different areas of social engagement: women prisoners; an ethnic minority; and young people in an inner-city parish. All three are areas of society that have known considerable suffering, and yet each story gives us hope that in such areas those who have hitherto been marginalized are now finding a new sense of value. Not only this, but we hear that those from the churches who are serving amongst these people are discovering Christ in a new way and experiencing a renewal of their faith.

Celia McCulloch is President of the Mothers' Union in the Wakefield Diocese and writes about a prison visiting initiative. By taking prayer, contemplation and worship into the darkness of imprisonment, Celia and the others with her have discovered unexpected wells of faith, hope and love. Although the focus has been to reach out to the inmates, it is the moving response of the prisoners that has brought renewal to the lives of the prison visitors. Jesus returned from the deserts of Judaea 'filled with the power of the Spirit . . . to proclaim liberty to the captives' (Luke 4.14, 18). Celia and her fellow visitors have witnessed the Spirit-inspired liberty being experienced by those in the captivity of prison.

The second story comes from *Pradip Sudra*, who is the Executive Secretary to the Alliance of Asian Christians. Pradip serves on various national councils including the Evangelical Alliance and the Board of Mission of the Church of England. His story is about the Asian Calvary Church in Wolverhampton. It is a story of a church coming to birth in the context of separation, pain and suffering and yet from the margins bringing renewal and hope to a city-centre church in Wolverhampton.

Our third story is by *Rob Burton*, who writes about the very creative *Zone Project* which is having a great impact on a Nottingham housing estate that has known considerable social deprivation. This story is about a church that has listened seriously to the local youth culture and sought a social and spiritual renewal for this wounded neighbourhood.

1. New Hall Women's Prison   *Celia McCulloch*

The work with inmates in New Hall Prison that the Mothers' Union in the Wakefield Diocese is doing did not start by accident. It is entirely the result of prayer. The prison already had a prison prayer chain and as the then chaplain was an MU member, she invited the members in the diocese to start praying for the work she was doing with the inmates. As we prayed for the chaplain we began to take a greater interest in her work there, and learnt of the need for a Mother and Baby Unit which would enable women to keep their babies with them in prison. And so a fundraising drive began which enabled the unit to receive baby equipment, books, toys and a special bag for each new baby, full of essential items – soap, creams, nappies, layette and a special toy just for them.

As a result of our prayers and fundraising efforts, the Mothers' Union was invited to the prison Carol Service in December 1994, where we met Jemima who had recently been transferred from Holloway prison. Jemima had joined the Mothers' Union in Holloway, and on seeing our MU badges immediately greeted us with joy and also asked why there was no branch in New Hall.

A branch in the prison seemed a wonderful opportunity to reach out and share our faith with this section of society, but it was a daunting task. If we began such a thing how on earth could we sustain it? What would our members think of it? A number of obstacles stood in our way (prison red tape being a significant one) but they were eventually overcome and we were finally given permission to hold monthly meetings in the prison. A branch was opened in May 1995; six members were enrolled into the Mothers' Union and one lady, a Hindu, was made an associate member.

Three 'outside' members became the meetings' leaders and, working with the prison chaplain, used the time to encourage self-awareness and a positive approach to how the inmates could continue to care for their families, especially their children, from inside by putting them in God's hands and trusting in him. Meetings always begin and end with prayer and this has enabled people to open up and share much more of their inner selves.

When one member, Kim, was due to be moved to another prison, in preparation for her final release, she was so overcome by what had happened to her through the loving, and entirely voluntary, support given to her by the 'outside' members that she wrote her own words to 'Amazing Grace' and sang them at her final service with the New Hall branch. On arriving at her new prison the first hymn she heard was 'Amazing Grace'! At the time of Kim's move we wrote to the Mothers'

Union in that diocese, commending her to them. They had no contact with the women's prison except through a couple of members who were general prison visitors. However, they made contact with Kim, and with her and the chaplain they too have now opened a Mothers' Union branch. Kim is now released and living in that part of the country. The Mothers' Union there continues to keep an eye on her and give her prayerful and practical support.

Due to prison transfers and releases, the branch at New Hall was eventually left without any MU members, but a group of inmates continued to meet each month led by the 'outside' members. Worship and singing have great meaning for them, and they often share their feelings about what the words mean to them. They sing their favourite songs and hymns in their cells, and one 'Lifers' cell has become a peaceful place of prayer and recollection for more recent inmates.

The MU has introduced quiet contemplative prayer, which has been a new experience for most. Yet participation has been heartfelt. Often, wonderfully, the prison corridors outside the chapel have fallen silent – a very rare and precious event. Prayer takes on a new dimension in this stripped-down place where life is often raw and basic.

We share news about our families and enjoy photos of new grandchildren or news of the latest phone call – sometimes a matter for rejoicing, sometimes for anger or frustration. Supporting and strengthening the family links is a vital lifeline, offering hope and an incentive to try to make good. Some come to see prison as the opportunity for a fresh start. All this is wrapped round in prayer – theirs and ours.

When the new chaplain decided to make Sunday services non-eucharistic, the first concern of these inmates was when and how they would be able to receive Holy Communion. As a result they turned to the MU, and now the monthly meetings centre on an informal and deeply meaningful celebration, which allows expression of real mutual love and care. There are lots of tears, especially at the intercessions (a box of tissues is always at hand, with sympathetic shoulders to cry on and arms to hug); but there is laughter too and a tremendous sense of hope, and faith that whatever happens in this life, we can all receive forgiveness through the cross.

Five more inmates have now joined the Mothers' Union and committed their lives to that missionary organization; but one has already moved to a prison nearer home, prior to discharge in a few months. There is a constant ebb and flow, but the message of love and care is moving out to other prisons and from there back into the community. The local 'outside' members continue to work with the inmates at the monthly meetings. Recently they together designed and made a banner proudly bearing the words 'New Hall Mothers' Union' in the freedom colours of red, green and yellow (a unique MU banner!). The dove, symbolizing the Holy Spirit, does not hover – it flies up and away – the banner is full of 'freedom' symbols. When the Bishop dedicated it he spoke of the real freedom in Christ, which took on new meaning in that setting.

They have also worked on creating an altar frontal for the chapel as an expression of their journey into faith. On a deep glowing-green background with gold borders is a gold cross. Beneath the cross there is a crowd of figures of all shapes, sizes and colours. Each of those involved drew a face on a figure which she chose, inmates, chaplain and 'outside' members; we are all there, equal before Jesus.

The work is small and low-key, but among other inmates there is a growing curiosity about what is happening, and the steady attendance of a dozen or so has suddenly begun to expand. Lives are being changed within the prison, and we, who now count them as friends, are experiencing fresh challenge and a renewed awareness of God's hand on our shoulders. We 'outside' members plan the content of meetings, but repeatedly have to respond to the unexpected – prisoners being unlocked very late, some having to leave part way through to attend an Alcoholics Anonymous meeting or drug counselling, a sudden influx of 30 when we had planned for 12, or perhaps 50 filling the chapel and entirely disrupting the planned programme by misbehaving. We have learned to say, 'Over to you, God!' and feel an increasing dependence on the Holy Spirit – only he knows what is happening. We very rarely feel as if we do, but somehow it doesn't matter.

We have been moved and humbled by the warmth and mutual love we have been allowed to share, and have delighted in signs of growing faith.

A special joy was provided by a long-serving prisoner who knitted a set of crib figures; each sheep had a different face, and the sheep closest to the crib was the black one. This prisoner has become a significant figure in many of our lives.

Our connection with the prison has changed us, and that change is obviously infectious. Other members in the wider diocese have been moved by our stories from inside. Twenty-six of them now visit the Mother and Baby unit on a weekly basis. They spend two or three hours of an afternoon or in the evening talking with the women, sewing, knitting and playing with the children. Recently permission has been given for these 'outside' members to take the children to the local village playgroup. Trust is being built up and slowly and gently, and mainly by example, they can begin to share their faith story.

To be allowed to share the inner struggles, joys and sorrows of these women is a privilege, and has led us all, freed from our separate prisons of isolation, self-concern and fear, further along the Way into the life of God. The experience of all the Christian folk who become involved in this work of trying to bring Jesus into the hearts of others so that they might be renewed, has been, in many different ways, truly enriched. To be engaged in this ministry has been truly an experience of renewal for us.

2. Asian community *Pradip Sudra*

The large-scale immigration of the Asian community into the UK from East Africa and the Indian subcontinent during the 60s and 70s has exposed them to the Christian Church in a way that was not possible in their own countries in the past. The number of people from other faith backgrounds becoming followers of Jesus Christ has grown. However, a survey conducted almost a decade ago concluded that seven out of ten people who came to faith in Christ from other faith backgrounds turned back to their former faith within the first year. The reason for this reversal was the lack of secondary support structures in the life of denominational churches. This situation gave rise to the creation of Alliance of Asian Christians (AAC), an umbrella body which seeks to encourage the development of the Asian Christian community. It does this by developing leadership and building structures which help discipleship and nurture in a culturally appropriate way. AAC also recognizes that the Asian Christian community is part of the wider Church and therefore efforts are made to build lasting relationship with all parts of the Church.

If moving home is one of the most stressful experiences, then moving to a new country, encountering a new race of people, a different language, a different religion and a different way of doing things must also rate as highly stressful. Amongst the new immigrants to the United Kingdom (most of whom were Hindu, Muslim and Sikh) there were a handful of Christians. They had to make sense of their lives in a new country and an important and unavoidable aspect was religion. Many went to the denominational churches with which they were affiliated in the Indian subcontinent. But they often encountered a lack of genuine welcome and the sheer *foreignness* of the language and culture. The need to worship in the language of one's heart and be a community led many to form prayer gatherings in their own front rooms. In the course of time these gatherings have become worshipping communities in their own right. Today, there are many congregations which are independent of denominations and equally there are those who have closer ties. This now settled community is developing relationships and the future is far more hopeful.

The Asian Calvary Church at St John's in Wolverhampton came to birth in rather difficult circumstances. The leader of this church, Revd Isaac Masih, and his core membership were part of another congregation in which he exercised a limited leadership role. There were many good things for which to commend this church, but it had a rather narrow understanding of ecclesiology and culturally it was frozen in the days of the British Empire – perhaps not surprising as the main leader was a former missionary to India.

There came a time when Isaac and some of the other members of the congregation were mature enough to work out for themselves the difference between what they read in their Bibles and the somewhat idiosyncratic leadership style of their minister. There were times when the minister would wave a £5 note and say to his congregation that this was their God. The implication of this kind of behaviour is rather offensive, and so, after much prayer and deliberation, they bid farewell to many people they loved and after a few weeks' break started to meet in their own homes. By March 1992 they had grown too large to hold meetings in their homes and a relationship was formed with St John's Church. At this stage there were about 30 people who worshipped together. Initially this relationship was only in the use of the building, but today it is a positive model of good partnership.

St John's Church is situated in a commanding position in the centre of town. However, it is surrounded by commercial enterprises (shops, offices, take-aways and night-clubs) and the regular congregation is ever diminishing. It would be fair to say that St John's is a typical inner-city church which is literally dying. The 1997 main Christmas service saw only 20 people (mainly Anglo-Saxons) in attendance. However, the attendance at the alternative Asian service topped the 200 mark.

The Bishop of Wolverhampton was amongst the first to recognize that renewal was on its way at St John's. What may originally have been seen as a convenient arrangement was God's unique provision for renewal. I believe it takes a prophet to recognize God's hand at work. The Bishop very helpfully and rather hopefully stressed that 'If the Asian church had not become part of St John then it was almost certain that a supermarket would have been trading in this building by now.'

Asian Calvary Church no longer meets in the adjacent hall – they have outgrown it and now meet in the main building. Almost a hundred worshippers of all ages turn out week after week to worship Jesus Christ. It is a unique experience to enter an Anglican church, with all its traditional furnishings, and find that the service is conducted in the Punjabi language (and translated into English). It is marvellous to hear new believers testifying to their new-found faith; their zeal is contagious. It truly is a testament of the older being renewed and the younger finding faith. Sixty per cent of the regular worshippers are under 40 years of age.

It is a sad fact of church life that whilst the Church is meant to be the only organization which exists for the benefit of its non-members, we become so comfortable in our routine and relationships that anything that threatens the *status quo* is resisted. When the Asian congregation moved from the smaller hall to the main church hall, serious jealousy emerged. The move was instigated by the Bishop because there was no logical reason for confining 100 people to a hall built for a smaller number, while a dozen people worshipped in a hall built to seat over 500. A number of racist comments were overheard but this discontent is settling with time. Combined meetings are still proving to be difficult because the styles of worship are not compatible and are felt to be too rigid. However, the vicar of the church, Revd Jonathan Hopcroft, is very hopeful about the future.

An activity of this growing church which has helped both congregations and many others in the town has been evangelistic missions which have emphasized physical and spiritual healing. The week-long meetings have seen up to 700 people of various ethnic origins packed into the church. Many have come to faith in Christ for the first time and many have also been physically healed. This activity has also created a deeper hunger for the word of God. Regular bible studies, prayer meetings and baptisms are also conducted.

A majority of those who have found faith in Christ come from Punjab (India) and they have been keen to go and share the Good News with their extended families. They have used their annual holidays to visit their relatives and friends and by travelling in teams have been extremely effective in sharing the Good News. Neither the language, the culture or the difficulty of getting around has hampered them, because they are operating with known boundaries. A group of lay people has visited Punjab annually and found that the congregations they helped to plant have grown considerably under local leadership and are in turn reaching out to others. The group was burdened to support the caretaker ministers in Punjab and to date they have part-supported seven ministers. One of the seven is now adequately supported by his own congregation and has requested that the support that he used to receive be earmarked towards another pioneering situation. It is hoped that this might be a theological training centre.

Members of the Asian Calvary Church who have been involved in outreach are certainly knowing renewal. There is a greater zeal and excitement in their own lives and worship. Ashok Masih (one of the leaders) claims that, in the process of taking the gospel to another part of the world, 'We have caught a greater vision to see all peoples renewed'. The weekly prayer meeting is a testament to what God can do with people who are willing to take risks. The last six years have done a number of things for this small congregation. The members believe that they can all adequately witness to their faith in Jesus Christ. Their worship has been broadened and deepened. They have taken responsibility for supporting their own minister and are beginning to develop leadership potential in others. They conclude by saying that renewal within has been as result of their involvement in mission – both at home and overseas.

3.   The Zone Youth Project   *Rob Burton*

The Broxtowe Estate is an outer-city housing estate on the NW edge of Nottingham City with a population of 7,000 people, of whom 45 per cent are under the age of 18 and 10 per cent of 10- to 15-year-olds have been in trouble with the police. High unemployment, high levels of youth crime, truancy and disaffection make the estate notorious. 1993 and 94 saw a period of heated antisocial conflict commonly called 'youth riots'. The images of mounted and riot police on the streets restoring order still live in the minds of people, refreshed periodically by the local newspaper suggesting that nothing much has changed on the estate. However, much has changed. Reversing negative labels and stereotypes is key to our work.

At the height of the disturbances a local radio phone-in programme broadcast the views of one young man: 'No one listens to us, no one cares, we're gonna show them. We're gonna fire bomb the community centre and the church. That'll make them listen . . .' No fire-bombs came but a public meeting called by the vicar, the Revd John Harding and his wife Ros, saw 30 local residents who were wrestling with the upheaval come together and share their stories of despair at what was happening. Ros believed deeply in community and knew that this was the answer to the heartfelt cry for 'someone to listen' which was a constant echo from young people. A year of listening to young people,

129

parents, community leaders and professionals helped to shape the necessary work which we believed would have a deep effect on the young people from our area. A visit by Bishop Patrick Harris, Bishop of Southwell, one December evening was the catalyst needed to embark on the Zone Youth Project.

Rob Burton, following a call to explore ministry, came to join the Hardings in their ministry in Broxtowe. During hours of discussion and prayer, often late into the night, the vision for the Zone Youth Project emerged and started to take shape. The vision called for a team of committed people, both local volunteers and skilled, experienced workers, to make this dream come into being. Playing an active part in the wider community's affairs helped to keep our finger on the pulse and secure credibility for the work we were doing. Five local people who joined Ros and Rob came to faith over this year. An application to the National Lottery Charities Board to fund a team of workers was successful and brought a real test of faith for those who felt called by God to this ministry. The funding carried an equal opportunities condition. All jobs would have to be advertised, interviewed and appointed under strict equal opportunities guidelines. After a day of prayer at Rempstone Convent to pray that God would bring about the appointment of a team who had a heart for young people and the skills necessary to bring about changed lives, came four months of interviews and appointments. The team appointed, including Ros and Rob, were committed Christians with a developed sense of God's call and purpose. The team consisted of a Co-ordinator, Drug Prevention Worker, Arts Development Worker, Schools Outreach and Streets Outreach workers, Dance Facilitator and another 12 volunteers from the local community. What follows is their story and how God has brought new life from a barren and dry place.

The Zone Youth Project, based in Broxtowe, Nottingham, works with young people aged fourteen and over, in schools, on the streets and in their homes. The Zone is an area-based project working across two other parishes, Aspley and Bilborough. Five secondary schools share young people from this area. Each week sees a programme of schools work including assemblies, issue-based workshops around themes such as bullying, conflict, truancy, careers, relationships etc., lunch-time discussions and mentoring support work. As well as this work in schools the Project is involved in regular drug prevention work, street football, sexual health drop-in and health information, dance groups, arts events, with 'pirate' radio DJs, a monthly youth newspaper called *The Pulse*, a drop-in café and getting alongside young people who simply need someone to care for them for a while.

During 1996 the work developed and was undergirded by prayer and worship. The Zone Team, all members of different churches, came together for worship and prayer each Sunday evening. A worshipping community was established and grew and became the foundation stone for the work among young people. Tragedy struck in April 1997 when Ros Harding died suddenly at the age of 49. Ros had created the project and was its co-ordinator. Trying to come to terms with the loss of a dear friend and colleague whose vision had given purpose and hope, trying to support the many young people who were heartbroken at the news, and the shock from the wider community who had come to know, love and respect Ros over the ten years she had lived in Broxtowe, could have overwhelmed the project and easily caused it to fold. The team met together during the days that followed the news. Shock, grief, despair, anger and tears overwhelmed any thought other than just being. Sometimes it would be too much to be together; sometimes John Harding would join us and we would share each other's grief. We sat in the vicarage lounge where so many of our team meetings and Sunday evenings had been spent.

In the days and weeks which followed we were all shocked at the depth at which Ros's death was felt by so many people. We were able to be part of the funeral service which saw nearly a thousand people come to Southwell Minster; young people were able to be part of that service, thanks to John and his family, and this helped them to start to come to terms with the loss. When the shock had started to diminish many in the community expected the Zone to end. They saw the work as being based around Ros's personality. We knew differently. It was a further shock to them, then, when we announced our plans for the next six months. One of these plans was to go ahead with a residential in July 1997. We knew that a residential would help to draw young people into the community formed by the team. We also knew that this community would need a sense of purpose and direction after the residential if it was going to last.

We had made a wonderful friendship with the Royal Philharmonic Orchestra and their Education Programme and before Ros's death had made a provisional date for them to be part of the ten-day residential, which would then be followed up during the autumn and winter of 97/98 with a tour to a couple of other areas. We knew that the residential and tour were a big step of faith; we had to be certain about what we were doing, certain that it was what God wanted us to do. I telephoned the RPO and we all agreed to go for it. We continued to worship and pray together. Three young people had become Christians and were joining us for our worship and prayer.

It would be easy to underestimate the enormity of the task we had set ourselves; Broxtowe is a community where some 33 per cent of households are led by a lone parent in receipt of benefit; 50 per cent of residents who are housed by the city council have been registered as homeless. For many of the young people we were taking away, this was their first holiday ever, never mind their first time away without a parent. This group were not performers or artists. They were urban young people who wanted to be able to express what life was like.

The aim of the residential was to produce a performance piece which would help them do just that. Working alongside the RPO were an African drummer, Ali Bangoura, and Janet Stickley from Nottingham's Footprints Theatre Company. It soon became obvious that many were finding it difficult to concentrate and fit in. They were having to face up to the fact that they could achieve something, when so often they had been conditioned into failure, perhaps through exclusion from school, the breakdown of family, or being in trouble with the police. Here was an experience which was proving that they could have faith in themselves and others; there was something to hope in, and that was starting to become uncomfortable and risky because it was new territory.

The programme gave a mixture of workshops, trips and outings – we all climbed Snowdon, a great achievement for many of the young people, and each evening we created a 'night-club' style event called 'The

Venue'. This was where the young people – and the team! – could chill out and relax. In the programme after each Venue at 11.30pm was the 'Late Night Mmm', a chance to let the still small voice of God be expressed among us. The first night at 11.30pm the Venue music stopped and about fifteen young people stayed for Late Night Mmm. Over the next few evenings more and more of the young people stayed for the Late Night Mmm. I asked one of my team, Mark, to share his faith story, which he did with a real humility and gentleness. I picked up on the main points of his story, that God could make a difference, that he had called each one of the young people here for a purpose, that he knew what they had been through and what they were feeling, that he wanted them to know the love he has for them. The Spirit of Jesus came down and started to touch these fragile young lives: some cried, some needed to be hugged, some just sat in the stillness. These young people were crying out to be helped. I invited the young people to receive prayer if they wanted it. Of the 35 young people who stayed on this particular night, 24 asked for prayer. I was amazed and humbled as I witnessed God healing broken lives.

The performance was ready and proved to be such a transforming moment for these young people; to achieve something which was beyond their horizon, a new experience, a natural high! The Lord was at work in the whole of what we were doing. It seemed such a natural way of things. The following evenings I shared my own faith story and spoke of the power of the cross, the freedom Jesus offers, the new life which is full of hope and purpose. Over the ten days eight young people made a faith commitment to follow Jesus; many more had started on a journey, all had experienced community and discovered that there was more to life than they had been led to believe.

I knew that at the heart of this experience was a deep sense of belonging and acceptance which was important for these young people. They had glimpsed a hope that they had not found before. One young person, Helen, asked if she could be baptized. Our local church had just been refurbished and had a newly-installed baptistery. The baptism was set for the last Sunday of October. I knew that the service would be an opportunity for God to move us on as a community. More young people had made commitments; again, more were seeking. The service consisted of a time of praise using 'sanctified dance music' and club-style lights and sound system. The baptistery was lit with candles; 60 young people came and about 30 adults. Peter Bailey, a priest from a neighbouring parish who has been a great encouragement to us (John Harding was on sabbatical) spoke about what Helen was doing at baptism. Helen shared her faith story and was then baptized.

It was an amazing experience, the more so because the water heater had not been connected so we were busy filling up the pool with a hose-pipe from the vestry for about six hours! I understand the water was still very cold! We welcomed Helen as a sister and again pushed back boundaries. 'I didn't realize church could be like this', said one young person who had been invited by Helen. Another young person said, 'When I was being prayed for I saw these lights, it was just like when I'd taken drugs except this time I hadn't. It was like Jesus saying to me "You don't need drugs any more".'

The community continues: 25 young people are meeting in cell groups weekly, we have a worship celebration each month, we meet all together once a month for a time of teaching and prayer. Everyone is using the same bible notes, and the cells spend time sharing what God has been saying, praying together and being there to support each other. We are being asked more and more to lead worship in other places; when we do, the whole community goes! Last week some of the guys spoke about their faith journey. The most poignant and moving was Chris, who said:

> I've been bad in the past. I've done house breaking
> and nicked cars, done drugs and the rest, but since I
> came into contact with the Zone, my life's changed.
> I haven't become a Christian, I'm still searching, like
> at a cross-roads. I hope I do become a Christian
> though.

The Zone Team continues with and is developing its weekly programme of schools work, which includes assemblies, issue-based workshops, lunch-time presentations and mentoring support work. Alongside this there is the regular drug prevention work, sexual health information, street football, dance groups, monthly arts events, *The Pulse* newspaper, a drop-in café, getting alongside young people who need someone to care for them for a while, and serving God where he has called us to be, doing what he has asked us to do. For all of us who are engaged in this work, it is an ongoing experience of renewal.

For reflection

1. Which of the three types of social action described above attracts you most?

2. What particular feature of the social action appeals to you?

3. Are there practical steps you can take to explore it further?

4. How do you feel about people in prison? Do you know much about your local prison? Is your church involved in any prison visiting?

5. If there is an ethnic minority community near you, how much do you know about it? How welcoming has your church been to those from other cultures who have moved in to your area? If you have people from ethnic minorities in your church, how relevant is the culture of the church to them?

6. As you think about Rob's story of the Zone Project, give some thought to the young people in your community. Give prayerful thought to whether your church might be able to spend time listening to God and the young people, to see if there may be appropriate ways of caring for them.

Resources

New Hall Women's Prison

For information about the Mothers' Union, write to: Mary Sumner House, 24 Tufton Street, London SW1P 3RB (Tel: 0171 222 5533/4/5).

Asian community

For information about the Alliance of Asian Christians, write to: Alliance of Asian Christians, Carrs Lane Church Centre, Carrs Lane, Birmingham B4 7SX (Tel: 0121 633 4533).

The Zone Youth Project

If you are interested in finding out more about the Zone Youth Project, a project outline, *The Pulse* youth newspaper and a prayer letter can be obtained from: Rob Burton, The Zone Youth Project, 137 Frinton Road, Broxtowe, Nottingham NG8 6GR.

9

Renewal across cultures

Introduction

The day of Pentecost described in Acts 2 is often seen as a model for spiritual renewal. The occasion was unique and the manifestation of the Spirit certainly unusual, but the experience of the spiritual empowering of God's people has been an important part of Christian spirituality. Pentecost hymns and prayers which invoke the coming of the Spirit recall the infant Church's first dramatic experience of it. Whilst many pentecostals and charismatics have rejoiced in the story, it has to be said that the significance of the multi-cultural aspect of Pentecost has often been overlooked. Luke, the writer of this account, makes very clear that 'there were devout Jews from every nation under heaven living in Jerusalem', and various national groups are identified as having heard the disciples speaking in their own languages. One of the gifts of Pentecost, therefore, is the gift of cross-cultural communication. From Pentecost we do not get an amorphous a-cultural group of people. We get a group of people who have had their own cultures affirmed by the fact that God has chosen to give their languages to the proclaiming evangelists. The really extraordinary part of the story is that the affirmation of each culture does not lead to independence, but to interdependence. The intercultural experience of the first part of chapter 2 leads to the expression of community that we read about in verses 44 to the end: 'All who believed were together and had all things in common.'

In this chapter we include some stories in which people have encountered a new and, to them, alien culture. The result of this encounter has been most definitely a renewing experience. *Bev Irving* is 25 years old and in 1997 took the opportunity to work short-term in India with a missionary society. She writes of her visit to a totally new culture and tells us about the inevitable vulnerability that this brings. Yet in the midst of it all she became open to the gifts of that culture and experienced the enfolding love of God.

Our second story is provided by *Revd Peter Swales* who is vicar of a parish just outside Derby. His church's decision to give hospitality to a Kenyan evangelist led to several of his church making a visit to Kenya in the summer of 1997. He describes how a group of fourteen from the parish made their first visit to Kenya, the impact that the visit made upon them, and the practical consequences of the relationship that has built up between the Derbyshire and Kenyan churches. As with Bev, the encounter with the two-thirds world engaged a wide range of emotions and a depth of experience that has changed lives.

Our third story is by *Revd David Truby*, another Derbyshire vicar, who tells us about the the link between Brimington and Staveley in the UK and Pfungstadt in Germany. This story takes us to cross-cultural encounters within Europe. He provides several short stories of those who have been involved in visits, both English and German, and these stories demonstrate not only the joy of renewal, but also the healing of reconciliation.

1.   Overseas Experience Placement (India)   *Bev Irving*

I have recently returned from six months in India, where I used my nursing skills on an Overseas Experience Placement facilitated by the Church Mission Society (CMS). When originally asked if I had a preference as to which country I might be sent, I didn't really have an answer. When India was suggested I was genuinely surprised because for some reason I'd imagined myself going to Africa or Eastern Europe.

I love talking about my experience! God prepared me well. I got kind support from CMS too. Though the flight was traumatic, I settled in India within a few days. I felt so many emotions, especially on my first day. Primarily, I was amazed at the sheer diversity of colour in a country filled with such dust, dirt and poverty. My senses felt constantly attacked, overwhelmed by the volume of noise and variety of smells.

During my time there I had numerous experiences which drew me closer to God, tested my faith and really opened my eyes, widening my train of thought. Within Britain we have great means of communication which enable us to visualize what happens in third world countries, but to have the opportunity to see those countries for yourself takes your perception a step further. I regularly thanked God for the opportunity he had given me to appreciate a new culture, to live with those shaped by it and learn from them.

At the centre of the Christian Medical Centre (CMC) Hospital in Vellore there is a chapel. It is said that if the chapel ever closed, then the hospital would quickly go too. It is the heart of the hospital, which was originally started by Dr Ida Scudder, a missionary from the USA. Every morning there is a worship service which nursing staff attend prior to their shift. Following that, on each ward the staff share a reading from the Psalms, pray for staff and patients, and give thanks to God. It was a wonderful start to the day.

CMC is very large, with 1,700 beds, and set in extensive grounds. There are always numerous relatives on the site as whole families may have come with each patient. One relative is requested to wash, dress and feed each patient. Outside visiting hours all the other relatives have to wait in allocated areas. They spill out into the corridors and literally camp outside the ward gates, which are held closed by security guards so that wards don't become overcrowded! Relatives follow their family member to surgery. Then they will sit and wait on the ground until they see the patient being pushed out on the trolley. Thirty relatives waiting outside an operating theatre is not uncommon.

I learnt that Indians are dedicated to their religion whether they are Muslims, Hindus or Christians, and that within their culture the family is essential. There were times when faith and family were combined, for example, on returning to the ward following major surgery, the patient, porter and myself are requested by the relatives to stop in front of the chapel doors. A prayer is said, perhaps a candle lit and then we are allowed to continue.

Revelation 7.9-17 indicates that in heaven there will be Christians from all over the world, and I have found that interaction with Indian Christians has broadened my horizons on Christian living. Their dedication to their faith and how they incorporate it into their lives has made a big impact on me.

It was encouraging to feel the obvious presence of God. I was blessed and tested. It enabled me to grow towards God with intensity and intimacy. Even when I experienced feelings of isolation I also felt that I was held up by the deep enfolding love of God.

2. Sharing of Ministries Abroad (Kenya) *Peter Swales*

It seems strange to think that before September 1996 I did not know that Anglican Renewal Ministries of the UK had a sister organisation in Kenya which operated under the title of ARK, or Anglican Renewal Kenya. Similarly, therefore, I did not know of the existence of Amos Wandera, their Director in Nairobi. In fact, there was so much that I did not know about Kenya and the work of ARK – but by the grace of God both I and the people in the parish of Horsley were soon to be educated! A phone call from the ARM office led to the parish offering to 'host' Amos for a few days prior to a conference they were organizing at Swanwick, just a few miles away, and to which several Kenyans had been invited.

His arrival in this country was complicated, because his departure had been delayed due to a mix-up over ticket arrangements; such was the love and affection that grew between Amos and Horsley parish that it was a pleasure and source of great excitement to raise the money to pay for the fare after just one appeal at a service during his stay. God knows when and how his people need to be motivated, and it was just one more confirmation that our relationship was as a result of divine intervention and planning. There was more to it than a short stay at the local vicarage with sundry acts of unreserved and mutually rewarding hospitality.

It is obvious in retrospect that our understanding of 'mission' was far too insular and, if we were to be honest, patronizing. We raised good sums of money for 'good causes' as lots of other churches do, and have had an ongoing 'active' relationship with a local Christian-based organization in Derby, to the extent that we have taken supplies to the centre – but rarely has there been hands-on involvement. All of that changed after the visit of Amos Wandera, and it may well have been God's unexpected way of motivating us to get into the fight personally – to become emotionally and practically involved, to be moved and disturbed by the needs of others, both at home and abroad.

It was exciting to receive an overseas guest, but we had to get the maps out to see where Kenya was on the African continent – be honest, do you know where it is exactly, without looking? A focus on the African state of Burkina Faso at Spring Harvest earlier that year had proven that we British know little about Africa, and probably other continents too, but the point was forcibly made by Amos's arrival. It is in East Africa, surrounded by Uganda, Tanzania, Ethiopia, Sudan and the Somali Republic – and the Indian Ocean!

We realize now how easy it is to raise money, send it to an agency in London using a box number, and then get on with church life. But our responsibility does not end there and therefore our corporate responsibility for our brothers and sisters in Christ living somewhere in the universal neighbourhood involves 24 hours a day, 7 days a week, 12 months a year prayer support at least – and preferably personal active knowledge and involvement too. With regard to Kenya, many of us are now interested in the political situation, tribal difficulties and complexities (although not enough to be experts), and the internal church activity, which has its own peculiarities!

Renewal is no longer a personal, local matter but a corporate and universal concern for me and the people of Horsley parish – a medium-sized rural area near Derby which had been blessed by the Holy Spirit in many ways, but especially with the introduction of the Alpha course, which had dramatic results in our parish. We had much to rejoice in, but we had become extremely busy. At the time of Amos's visit, the pace was taking its toll and some were feeling the pressure on their health, family life, response to work situations, different ministries within the local church itself, and adapting to change.

Renewal had come to the parish church and its effects were showing outside the church too, which was frightening to some, a source of threat to others, and the signal to oppose it, come what may, to yet others. Irrespective of their opinions on renewal, everyone was affected and impressed by Amos Wandera and his infectious joy and enthusiasm for the love of God and his many blessings in difficult situations. His energetic, but not always accurate guitar playing was great fun – although I had some reservations with his after-midnight and very early morning practising in the next room at home! He introduced praise songs in a different language, Swahili, with words that allowed us to share the joy, somehow knowing what they meant. Before his flight back to Nairobi, he dropped into a conversation the invitation for me, and per-haps a team – including musicians, with whom he had built up a special affinity (and they with him!) – to attend the next conference of ARK in Kenya the following year.

I almost jokingly mentioned it to the congregation and was astonished to find that not only did they think it a good idea for me to go, but also Ann, my wife, and a team – including musicians. It proved how little they, and I, knew about Kenya – the logistics of taking a team across country is somewhat more complicated than driving from Derby to, say, Liverpool. The practical difficulties were for another day; God had spoken – we appreciate that in retrospect for sure, but also felt it to be the case from the beginning! Call it discernment – why not, that's what it was!

We received great help in planning our trip from SOMA (Sharing of Ministries Abroad), an international organization which enables small teams to visit other countries. Its present Director, Revd Don Brewin, has become a friend and welcome visitor here, and his unstinting and quite selfless encouragement and wise advice proved invaluable time and again. Don guided us through all manner of situations that had to be faced, dealt with, overcome, avoided or removed. It is not easy to discuss plans with the lovely, loving, and otherwise co-operative people from another continent and culture, using communications that don't always work. Telephones in Kenya often do not ring, and fax machines fool you into believing that messages have been received when they have not; e-mail is available and we used it, but answers never came back via the same route. People speak English in Kenya as a second language, and that is a relief when you do not speak any Swahili, but they have a heavy accent, speak fast, and use terminology which is not necessarily natural to us. Nobody's fault, but sometimes problematic, and potentially embarrassing – we took on far more than we could have been expected to achieve on a first visit to Africa, but God is good and big enough to deal with the most naive travellers abroad.

No matter how mature we feel spiritually, as Christians it takes a pilgrimage or mission trip to another culture to strip us of our pride and arrogance. It happened in 1994 when a party from Horsley went to the Holy Land and saw not only the religious tourist spots, but also how Palestinians live as Christians or Muslims alongside Jews religious and secular (mostly the latter) in conditions that shock the first-time visitor and at a pace that frustrates Westerners in particular. If it is important enough to do it today, then why not wait until tomorrow and maybe do it better!

East Africa is even more of a shock; no matter how hard and skilfully Don Brewin prepared us; no matter how carefully we listened to Bishop Bob Beak, a retired bishop who served in Kenya and now lives in Derbyshire whilst maintaining active links with the country; no matter how many books we read and documentaries we watched on television; we were simply not ready for Kenya 1997 – and the conditions in which its people live.

In the Diocese of Derby right now we are experiencing a time of review as a response to falling clergy numbers – the present more than 200 clergy posts will have to fall by the year 2000 to something nearer 180, and parishes will have to work together. Easier said than done. Not our fault, of course, because it is what we have become used to; but in Kenya we met an Anglican clergyman who has a 'parish' geographically bigger in size than the whole of Derby Diocese (which covers most of the county) and no car or other source of personal transport to help his ministry. In addition, he has a diocesan position – and his smile was as big as a fortnight!

Stipends are often irregular. Amos was ordained in December 1996 and has recently moved to the western diocese of Bungoma to take up a parish, a diocesan position and the supervision of a project within the community – all without any payment for him or his wife and two small children. He accepted it on those terms and sees it as a test of his faith.

As an aside, the house he has been allocated is rundown, has no generator (the cost to repair it is beyond the diocese's means at the equivalent of £50) and no facilities like electricity, water, sanitation, etc.

It was into this East African simplicity that we, a team of fourteen, arrived in August 1997, staying in Nairobi, receiving the generous hospitality of local Christians for a few days, and being told how grateful they all were for the way Amos had been received and treated by us. From there we travelled west to Lubinu High School in the diocese of Mumias to share in the week-long conference organized by ARK. The ten-hour road journey by coach was arduous and tested our new-found gift of patience. The conditions were primitive by Nairobi standards, let alone ours, and we were actually pleased to get back to Nairobi after the conference for 'a touch of luxury' before returning to England! Please do not ask what the 'long drop' system of sanitation means because you would not be comfortable with the reply!

The conference itself, however, was a joy and an education. We learnt not simply to listen to God, but to go with what we heard despite local opposition and spiritual warfare in the shape of the most unexpected people; they themselves may not be aware of their role in the war! The ARK conference is a time of spiritual refreshment for parched pastors and lay people alike, after a hard year in the battlefield; understandably it becomes a time for letting the hair down! Yet I felt led to speak about finding the Holy Spirit in the quiet places, using spiritual exercises that were unfamiliar and hitherto inappropriate – I felt quite out of place sharing a platform with American and Australian evangelists who were gifted in their teaching, but far from quiet! To follow that was daunting, but here was the test of renewal – it means not only praise songs but facing the hard places. I was taking them into the hurting areas but felt assured that God was using me to offer healing, vision and alternative ministerial styles. I lost a lot of sleep at first, especially before flying out, when I realized what God was asking of me; but I slept well afterwards!

The effect was immediate, with pastors in particular appreciating the opportunity to find their own 'quiet place' and develop a deeper, personal and more intimate relationship with Christ through the Holy Spirit in their own room, outside at dawn (well, it was Africa!), under the shade of a tree, during a walk, or even in a packed plenary room with almost 1,000 'travellers along the Way' in close proximity.

We even introduced 'the holy massage' – a neck or shoulder rub for your neighbour whilst telling them that Jesus loves them very much indeed. Perhaps you needed to be there to fully appreciate that one! However, Bishop William gave me the privilege of leading the final prayer on the last evening of the conference – at 12.15am after a four-hour service including communion – and as I did so, the people asked for the holy massage. It was surely for remedial purposes after such a long stint, but I took it as a compliment. The evening was memorable for a sad reason too, because it was the day Princess Diana was killed in France, and the news saddened Africa as much as England because she had done so much to champion the cause of the underprivileged and voiceless – not least in her campaign against the use of land mines, which have been such a blight on the African continent.

We made many new friends in Africa, and have struck up correspondence with dozens since returning. Some of these are known personally to us by name and face, such as our hosts and contacts at Greenfields Christian centre in Nairobi, where Amos and his wife Jane used to work until moving to Bungoma, along with the inspirational Revd Gilbert Amimo and his wife Dorna, who sadly died a few weeks after our return to England.

Many unknown children were introduced to us at the Mercy Care Centre in Mathare, Nairobi by Mama Amimo, whose vision and response to the love of God it is. Mathare is a shanty town of unbelievable deprivation, unless you have been there; to live there is our worst possible nightmare! A few miles from the wealthy suburbs and city centre of Nairobi, the roads into Mathare valley are mud tracks, just wide enough for a vehicle but by no means made for one. Along the side of the track run open sewers with shacks made of any materials alongside; there food is stored (such as it is) and cooked on open fires. Children run in groups, unprotected from any dangers, usually from single-parent families with teenage mums who live by prostitution and escape from the harsh realities and apparent imprisonment of their lives by solvent abuse.

All education in Kenya has to be paid for and proceeds as finances allow, so grades often have wide age ranges – no money, no school. In Mathare there is a small school catering for a few children and with an unfathomable selection process. Mama Amimo saw the need for Christians to finance another free school for the rest, so some 300 primary children receive free education from volunteer teachers in Dickensian conditions. No desks, pencil stubs around their necks on string, few books to write on, none to read from and poor light. When possible, they feed the children too! That is an expensive addition to their aim, because even basic foods are expensive and subject to harvest price-swings.

When we went there, each member of the team was visibly and profoundly affected; deeply stirred and yet unable to help in a practical way. The system is alien to us, and yet we all knew we had to do something. Initially, this was to offer the gifts of basic equipment we had taken, having heard from Amos about the school – although he did not tell us how bad it was. How could he? Amos is Kenyan, and not a wealthy one either, so the conditions are not that appalling to him – we had to see it for ourselves and feel the pain.

Our response may well have been guilt, self-pity, indignation, anger, or inadequacy; it may have been admiration, moral support, realization of our neighbours' plight; or it may have been renewal, the Spirit of God stirring us at the deepest emotional and spiritual level to see life and its conditions, and the way that God had decided we needed to go as his chosen and adopted children. *The Message* interprets John 1.14 as follows: 'The Word became flesh and blood, and moved into the neighbourhood.' In Mathare, we saw the incarnation at work in the loving response of Mama Amimo, Felix the young head-teacher, his volunteer (qualified) teaching colleagues and the support from local Christians who share their income with the project, even though they can scarcely manage themselves. We have done what we can do immediately and responded to a cash flow crisis, but in the longer term we are aiming to sponsor young people to go to Mathare and work there for six months or a year, help to improve the teaching conditions, sponsor children and staff in order to share the burden with the local Christians, and perhaps raise the funds and technical know-how to construct a school facility in the area. Some aspects are nearer being put into action than others, but all are possible, and if it is God's will (and we perceive that it is), it will happen to his glory!

Our return home has been uncomfortable, with all sorts of manifestations of dis-ease among the team – illness, disillusionment at work, pressure in the family, church ministries being reviewed, and brains taxed as to how, exactly, we should be living our lives. What has God done with us, and what is he saying to us, individually and corporately? This is renewal, but not in the way any of us envisaged that it would come – no hands-on ministry, no heavenly choruses, no obvious signs of change in church life, no massive increases in attendances at services (the reverse in some cases!) – and no sense of peace; just a knowledge that a deep spiritual activity is occurring and the ramifications are yet to be clarified.

'The case continues . . .' as they say in all good novels; and the catalyst for all of this was and is Amos Wandera, our friend in Kenya with whom we have a relationship like no other. When he was here in 1996, I took him to the local primary school where black faces are rarely seen, and he talked for some time while the children listened in awestruck silence. Afterwards one of the children came to me and said, 'Mr. Swales, is Amos an angel?' I had no answer to that because I have never, consciously, met an angel, but I have often wondered since! For me, and indeed for Horsley Church, he has performed the same duties – messenger and comforter. We are currently discussing where we go from here, and whatever comes out of those discussions, we will move on – safe in the knowledge of God's Spirit and his renewing power, but with the dream that it will overflow into revival so that all may share the privilege of knowing a closer relationship with the Father, and enjoying a glimpse of heaven here on earth. Alleluia!

3.   A cross-cultural link (Germany)   *David Truby*

The link between these two areas is both ecumenical and cross-cultural. The churches in Brimington and Staveley initiated the link nearly 26 years ago through the work of Revd Kenneth Mowl, the then minister of Staveley Methodist Church. From the outset, members of other

churches were involved, though over the years those who have participated have been either Methodist or Anglican. The German Parish of
Pfungstadt is part of the Evangelishe Kirche Deutschland, and serves a
small town near the city of Frankfurt.

Over the 25 years of the link, a friendship has grown between our two
peoples which has had considerable influence in the life of our respective
churches. The annual meetings give a wider understanding of one
another and lead to a community where ecclesiastical and national borders mean little. There is a wonderful sense of belonging to each other
and a desire to support each other in many ways, particularly prayer.

It is encouraging to think that such a link has been maintained over the
years, and that it is being continually strengthened by the numbers of new
people who become involved. The past two years have seen groups of over
thirty people visiting either England or Germany. Each time, those who
visit are accommodated in the homes of people in the respective parishes.

When I first came to the parish it was mentioned that there was a link
between us and one of the churches in Germany. Someone forgot to tell
me that if I visited with the group, then I would be expected to preach in
German on the Sunday that we were there! Fortunately, I had done a bit
of German at school and my hosts were very good at helping me put it
right the night before it was due to be preached.

I wasn't sure what to expect when I first took part in a visit. It would be
nice to have a holiday in Germany, and it would be good for our children
to have some experience first hand of life in another country, but I realized before long that it was much more than a bit of ecumenical
tourism. There is a great sense of being part of a family whenever we
meet, even though a number of those present will be joining in for the
first time. People are at ease with each other and there is always a lot of
laughter, a sure sign that God is in the midst!

Many of those who take part have memories of less happy times and of
conflicts between our two countries, and it is those people who have
most impressed me by their participation. They have put aside those
memories and, through being a part of the link, have experienced a real
sense of healing of past wounds.

For our younger people, there is the knowledge that they may be of different nationalities, but they are still part of a community of nations to which they belong. Above all, though, I have been very much aware of what it means to be a part of the Body of Christ. Our worship together may be in two languages, but there is the language of love which underlies it all.

I have found that my experience of the link has deepened this understanding that the Christian faith does not recognize boundaries of nationality. Opportunities to talk to fellow clergy in Germany and share something of their concerns for the future of the Church there mean that it is possible to have a wider view of what it means to be the Church. To show how it is possible for a church to thrive without the benefit of church tax and to share something of the breadth of tradition that exists within the Church of England, these are all little things which help to build the bond between us and have a wider understanding of the Church of Christ and its mission to the world.

It would be wrong of me to give the impression that all the members of the churches involved are keen to be part of the link. There will always be those who find it hard to forgive what they see as past wrongs. There will be those too who are simply indifferent. It can be difficult to find homes for our guests to stay in, and I know that the same problem is also experienced in Germany. A whole week is a long time to have strangers come to stay who may not even speak the same language as you. Those who have been persuaded always come back for more, though!

Despite the problems that we do face sometimes, I feel that the link has deepened and enriched the lives of our local churches. An interesting 'spin off' is that it has been one way in which all the local churches have been able to work together. The co-operation needed has led to a better ability to work together in other areas too, and so, indirectly, everyone benefits.

The rest of this contribution is written by three people who have taken part in the link. The two German contributions are reprinted from a pamphlet entitled *In One Spirit Joined*, published to celebrate the 25th Anniversary of the link.

Irmgard Brunner from Pfungstadt

At the beginning of our relationship with England there were mixed feelings. Many of us had experienced the War as young adults. This was only 25 years ago and still part of us. We were very doubtful and just couldn't eliminate the past. We had lost brothers, fathers and husbands; our cities had been laid in ruins and ashes, and we could only save our bare lives. We were aware of our immense debt. How could we face our former enemies? How could we look into their eyes?

I think these similar thoughts were also going through the minds of those who came from England, yet you, like our party, were prepared to stretch out your hands to receive us as friends. I came with the first party in 1973 and I don't forget the nights when we returned from our meetings and continued talking for hours and tried to explain how we experienced the horror of war and how important it was for us that people were talking to us again and wanted to be friends, sisters or brothers. We were overwhelmed by so much love and kindness.

For me, and I think also for those who have been visiting each other, this coming together means a valuable enrichment of our parish life and our understanding of what it means to be a Christian. We learnt so much and thank God for the experience with good friends, surpassing all borders.

Alexander Eich from Pfungstadt

I am now 18 years old and it was five years ago now that a school friend asked me whether I was interested in an exchange of our Protestant church with the English parishes of Brimington and Staveley. As I knew the English way of living and culture from school, books and TV only, I decided to take part in the exchange. A few months later another young student and I found ourselves in the room of the children of our hosts, who welcomed us heartily. It was not difficult to meet 'real' young English people and to become friends because that very year many young people joined the party from Pfungstadt.

My father too, also stayed with a couple in Brimington, and made friends with his and other English hosts very quickly. In general, I had the impression that there were no language barriers and we always found a way to make ourselves understood, if necessary without the medium of language. I noticed during the whole visit that it was above all filled with feelings like interest, tolerance and friendship which our society today could take as an example.

Mary Webb from Brimington

In 1975, the Pfungstadters visited us here in England, and the customary service was held at our church here in Brimington. Inspired by the sense of belonging to each other despite our different languages and church traditions, I felt drawn towards the group and so went on my first visit to Pfungstadt in May 1976. We travelled by train to Harwich, by ferry to the Hook of Holland and on the Rhine Express to Darmstadt where our hosts met us with their cars.

I had been looking forward to the visit with anticipation and some dread since I am naturally a reserved person. My hostess was a lady who had many responsibilities in the church, and lives in one of the oldest houses remaining in Pfungstadt, dating from the seventeenth century. I was made very welcome by the family (including the dog!). Frau Brunner could speak some English and I could speak a little German, and having been born in the same year meant that a bond was formed which has stood the test of time.

She had lived in the nearby town of Darmstadt during the War and was there when it was destroyed by bombing which was, I understand, quite unnecessary. We talked about the war and the suffering caused in Germany, Britain and other countries involved. The subject still comes up in conversations with some of the older people in Pfungstadt, always with the conviction that it must never happen again.

I have visited Pfungstadt seven times since that first visit. People are so friendly that it now seems like a second home. Though the expression of worship is different, there is a strong sense of being one in Christ. Living with families as we do has brought us together in friendship, fellowship and understanding, making us feel very positively members of the one family of God.

For reflection

1. Which of the three types of cross-cultural encounter described above attracts you most?

2. What particular feature of this encounter appeals to you?

3. Are there practical steps you can take to explore it further?

4. If you have visited other cultures, what has been your instinctive response – curiosity? Fear? Excitement?

5. What do you feel other cultures offer that your culture cannot?

6. Are you aware of still being suspicious of some other cultures because of previous conflicts? Can you think of ways of seeking reconciliation?

Resources

Overseas Experience Placement (India)

Short-term placements are arranged by various mission societies. Among them are: CMS, 157 Waterloo Road, London SE1 8UU (Tel: 0171 928 8681; Fax: 0171 401 3215) and USPG, 157 Waterloo Road, London SE1 8UU (Tel: 0171 928 8681).

Sharing of Ministries Abroad (Kenya)

For details of SOMA UK, write to: The Director, Revd Don Brewin, PO Box 6002, Heath and Reach, Leighton Buzzard, LU7 0ZA (Tel: 01525 237953; Fax: 01525 237954; e-mail: SOMAUK@compuserve.com).

A cross-cultural link (Germany)

Details about the Staveley/Brimington-Pfungstadt Link can be had from: Revd David Truby, The Rectory, Church St., Brimington S43 1JG. Further information about the Church and Europe can be sought from: CAFE (Christianity and the Future of Europe), c/o Westcott House, Cambridge CB5 8BP.